Springer Briefs in Criminology
Policing

SpringerBriefs in Criminology present concise summaries of cutting edge research across the fields of Criminology and Criminal Justice. It publishes small but impactful volumes of between 50-125 pages, with a clearly defined focus. The series covers a broad range of Criminology research from experimental design and methods, to brief reports and regional studies, to policy-related applications.

The scope of the series spans the whole field of Criminology and Criminal Justice, with an aim to be on the leading edge and continue to advance research. The series will be international and cross-disciplinary, including a broad array of topics, including juvenile delinquency, policing, crime prevention, terrorism research, crime and place, quantitative methods, experimental research in criminology, research design and analysis, forensic science, crime prevention, victimology, criminal justice systems, psychology of law, and explanations for criminal behavior. SpringerBriefs in Criminology will be of interest to a broad range of researchers and practitioners working in Criminology and Criminal Justice Research and in related academic fields such as Sociology, Psychology, Public Health, Economics and Political Science.

More information about this series at https://link.springer.com/bookseries/11179

Sanja Kutnjak Ivković • Jon Maskály
Ahmet Kule • Maria Maki Haberfeld

Police Code of Silence in Times of Change

Sanja Kutnjak Ivković
School of Criminal Justice
Michigan State University
East Lansing, MI, USA

Jon Maskály
Department of Criminal Justice
University of North Dakota
Grand Forks, ND, USA

Ahmet Kule
Department of Social, Cultural, and
Justice Studies
University of Tennessee at Chattanooga
Chattanooga, TN, USA

Maria Maki Haberfeld
John Jay College of Criminal Justice
City University of New York
New York, NY, USA

This book is an open access publication.

ISSN 2192-8533　　　　　　ISSN 2192-8541　(electronic)
Springer Briefs in Criminology
ISSN 2194-6213　　　　　　ISSN 2194-6221 (electronic)
Springer Briefs in Policing
ISBN 978-3-030-96843-4　　　ISBN 978-3-030-96844-1　(eBook)
https://doi.org/10.1007/978-3-030-96844-1

With the support of more than 30 libraries, the LYRASIS United Nations Sustainable Development Goals Fund has enabled this publication to be available fully open access.

© The Author(s) 2022
Open Access This book is licensed under the terms of the Creative Commons Attribution 4.0 International License (http://creativecommons.org/licenses/by/4.0/), which permits use, sharing, adaptation, distribution and reproduction in any medium or format, as long as you give appropriate credit to the original author(s) and the source, provide a link to the Creative Commons license and indicate if changes were made.
The images or other third party material in this book are included in the book's Creative Commons license, unless indicated otherwise in a credit line to the material. If material is not included in the book's Creative Commons license and your intended use is not permitted by statutory regulation or exceeds the permitted use, you will need to obtain permission directly from the copyright holder.
The use of general descriptive names, registered names, trademarks, service marks, etc. in this publication does not imply, even in the absence of a specific statement, that such names are exempt from the relevant protective laws and regulations and therefore free for general use.
The publisher, the authors and the editors are safe to assume that the advice and information in this book are believed to be true and accurate at the date of publication. Neither the publisher nor the authors or the editors give a warranty, expressed or implied, with respect to the material contained herein or for any errors or omissions that may have been made. The publisher remains neutral with regard to jurisdictional claims in published maps and institutional affiliations.

This Springer imprint is published by the registered company Springer Nature Switzerland AG
The registered company address is: Gewerbestrasse 11, 6330 Cham, Switzerland

To Zoran and Dora for showing me what love is (again!).

Sanja Kutnjak Ivković

To my family, friends, and colleagues for supporting me in my endeavors.

Jon Maskàly

For my wife Burcin and children Elif, Miray, and Ekrem.

Ahmet Kule

To all the good cops out there who put their lives on line every day to protect us, and to my daughters, Nellie and Mia, and my grandchildren, Amelia and Jordan, who continue to be my guiding lights.

Maria Maki Haberfeld

Contents

1	**The Pressing Need to Study the Code of Silence**	1
	Introduction	1
	The Code of Silence	4
	The Code of Silence and the Theory of Police Integrity	5
	Measuring the Code of Silence	7
	Police Officer Sample	9
	Overview of the Book	10
	References	12
2	**The Code of Silence and the Theory of Police Integrity**	17
	Introduction	17
	Studying the Code of Silence	18
	Correlates of the Code of Silence	20
	Organizational Correlates	20
	Individual Correlates	21
	This Chapter	22
	Methodology	22
	Sample	22
	Measures	22
	Analytic Strategy	24
	Results	25
	Contours of the Code of Silence	25
	The Effects of Police Integrity Measures on the Code of Silence	27
	Conclusion	30
	References	32
3	**The Code of Silence and Disciplinary Fairness**	37
	Introduction	37
	Discipline Fairness and Police Integrity	38
	Theoretical Approaches	39
	Empirical Measurement of Discipline Fairness	40

	Studying the Relationship Between the Code of Silence	
	and Perceptions of Disciplinary Fairness	41
	This Chapter	42
	Methodology...	42
	Sample...	42
	Measures...	42
	Analytic Strategy	44
	Results..	44
	The Effects of Discipline Fairness on the Code of Silence.........	44
	The Effects of Discipline Fairness and Police Integrity	
	Measures on the Code of Silence	48
	Conclusion	52
	References...	53
4	**The Code of Silence and Organizational Justice**	57
	Introduction...	57
	Organizational Justice.......................................	58
	Effects of Organizational Justice on Police Attitudes and Behavior....	59
	Organizational Justice and the Code of Silence	61
	This Chapter	62
	Methodology...	62
	Sample...	62
	Measures...	62
	Analytic Strategy	65
	Results..	65
	The Effects of Organizational Justice on the Code of Silence	65
	The Effects of Organizational Justice and Police Integrity	
	on the Code of Silence	66
	Conclusion	70
	References...	72
5	**The Code of Silence and Self-Legitimacy**	77
	Introduction...	77
	Self-Legitimacy...	78
	Effects of Self-Legitimacy on Police Attitudes and Behavior	80
	Self-Legitimacy and the Code of Silence	81
	This Chapter	82
	Methodology...	83
	Sample...	83
	Measures...	83
	Analytic Strategy	85
	Results..	85
	The Effects of Self-Legitimacy on the Code of Silence	85
	The Effects of Self-Legitimacy and Police Integrity on to the Code	
	of Silence	85
	Conclusion	90
	References...	92

6	**Lessons Learned About the Code of Silence**............................	95
	Introduction...	95
	Disciplinary Fairness and Organizational Justice.......................	97
	Organizational Justice and Self-Legitimacy...............................	99
	Disciplinary Fairness and Self-Legitimacy.................................	101
	This Chapter...	102
	Methodology...	102
	Sample..	102
	Measures..	102
	Analytic Strategy...	104
	Results...	104
	The Effects of Police Integrity, Distributive Fairness, Organizational Justice, and Self-Legitimacy on the Code of Silence................	104
	Conclusion...	109
	References...	114
Index...		119

About the Authors

Sanja Kutnjak Ivković is Professor in the School of Criminal Justice, Michigan State University. Dr. Kutnjak Ivković is also currently serving as the Chair of the American Society of Criminology, Division of International Criminology. Her research focuses on comparative and international criminology, criminal justice, and law. She received the 2017 Mueller Award for Distinguished Contributions to International Criminal Justice. Dr. Kutnjak Ivković has co-authored or co-edited ten books, including *Police Integrity in South Africa* (2020), *Exploring Police Integrity* (2019), *Measuring Police Integrity* (2015), *Enhancing Police Integrity* (2006), *The Fallen Blue Knights: Controlling Police Corruption* (2005), and *Contours of Police Integrity* (2004). Her work has appeared in leading academic and law journals such as the *Law and Society Review*; *Journal of Criminal Law and Criminology*; *Criminology and Public Policy*; *Law and Policy*; *Stanford Journal of International Law*; *Cornell International Law Journal*; *Crime, Law, and Social Change*; *European Journal of Criminology*; *Policing and Society*; *Policing: An International Journal*; *Police Quarterly*.

Jon Maskály is Assistant Professor in the Department of Criminal Justice at the University of North Dakota. Dr. Maskály is currently the President of the Southwestern Association of Criminal Justice. His research focuses on factors that affect police-community relationships, comparative policing, and quantitative methods. He has authored more than 30 peer-reviewed journal articles that have appeared in journals including *Crime and Delinquency*, *Journal of Interpersonal Violence*, *Social Science Research*, *Journal of Criminal Justice*, *Policing: An International Journal*, and *Policing and Society*.

Ahmet Kule is Assistant Professor of Criminal Justice in the Department of Social, Cultural, and Justice Studies at the University of Tennessee Chattanooga. He received his master's degree (2005) and doctorate (2007) in criminal justice from the City University of New York. Ahmet Kule served with the Turkish National Police at various ranks for 15 years. Later, he served at the NATO School in Germany as a senior instructor for 8 years. Dr. Kule developed and taught 10 different courses on national security, and trained more than a 1000 officers from 30 different countries during these 8 years. He also taught at several other institutions, including Center of Excellence (NATO-Ankara), John Jay College of Criminal Justice, and Montclair State University. He primarily teaches both graduate and undergraduate courses in terrorism, homeland security, cybercrime, policing, hate crimes, justice policies, and comparative criminal justice. Dr. Kule has published two books and several journal articles on national security, terrorism, radicalization, policing, criminal interrogations, corrections, and unmanned aerial systems.

Maria Maki Haberfeld is Professor of Police Science at John Jay College of Criminal Justice in New York City. She holds a PhD in criminal justice from the City University of New York. She served in the Israeli Defense Forces in a counterterrorist unit and left the army at the rank of a Sergeant. Later she served in the Israel National Police and left the force at the rank of Lieutenant. She is one of the founders of Police Leadership Program for the NYPD sworn officers and the academic director of this program since its creation in 2001. In addition, she has created the Law Enforcement Leadership Institute for Police Chiefs in New York State and created an online Law Enforcement Leadership Certificate. She has trained police forces around the country and the world, including the Dominican Republic, Czech Republic, Poland, India, China, Cyprus, Turkey, Mongolia, and Taiwan, and conducted research in over 70 police departments in the USA and in 35 other countries. She has published 21 academic books on policing and over 50 book chapters and journal articles in peer-reviewed publications. Her books were translated into 3 languages and are used by police departments around the country and around the world.

Chapter 1
The Pressing Need to Study the Code of Silence

Abstract This chapter summarizes the most recent calls for defunding and reforming police organizations around the country. A number of high-profile cases that focused primarily on the alleged notions of excessive use of force contributed to the explosion of criticism of the legitimacy of police actions. No time has been more critical in terms of the study of police integrity than now. This importance is further underscored by the need to connect the public outcry, mostly based on anecdotal accounts of police performance, to empirical research that has been in existence for over two decades and has produced valuable and implementable solutions. The pressing need to study the nature of the police code of silence and its resistance to change will be illustrated by our analyses of one case study, expanding the traditional police integrity framework developed by Klockars and colleagues in the past two decades.

Keywords Code of silence · Police integrity · Police misconduct · Theory of police integrity · Questionnaire · Survey · Police officers

Introduction

Studying police integrity and police misconduct has been a steady staple of learning about the policing profession for quite a few decades now, including the seminal works of Maurice Punch (1985, 2000, 2009), Jerome Skolnick (2002), O.W. Wilson (Cohen & Taylor, 2014), Kappeler et al. (1998), David Bayley and Robert Perito (2011), Sam Walker (2012), Klockars et al. (1997, 2000, 2004, 2006), and, most recently, Geoffrey Alpert and Kyle Mclean (2021). Numerous high-profile scandals shook the American public in the past few decades, including the infamous Rodney King beating caught on a video camera in 1991, as well as more recent events, such as the shooting of Michael Brown (Ray et al., 2017), the death of Eric Garner (Fulton-Babicke, 2018), and the brutal death of George Floyd (Samayeen et al., 2020). These scandals resulted in the creation of some high-profile commissions such as the Warren Commission (Goldsmith, 2005), the Christopher Commission

© The Author(s) 2022
S. Kutnjak Ivković et al., *Police Code of Silence in Times of Change*,
SpringerBriefs in Criminology, https://doi.org/10.1007/978-3-030-96844-1_1

(1991), the Mollen Commission (1994), and, more recently, President's Task Force on 21st Century Policing (2015). The establishment of these commissions has been preceded with public revelations of police misconduct of individual police officers, the so-called "bad apples." These revelations prompted the city governments to establish the commissions and empower them to investigate the nature and extent of police misconduct, as well as to propose ways in which the police agency could be reformed. These events have also resulted in a number of Consent Decrees negotiated between the Department of Justice and police agencies (Rhodes et al., 2019; Alpert et al., 2017). Consent decrees, based on "pattern and practice lawsuits" in which the Department of Justice is one of the parties, have been used as a tool to reorganize the departments based on the findings of the external monitors.

In the aftermath of these high-profile incidents, the focus seemed to be primarily on the individual police officers involved; only more recently did the focus shift on the organization itself, or, even more broadly, the police profession as a whole. The scope and magnitude of calls for reform have intensified in the wake of high-profile deaths at the hands of the police. Yet, as was the case with prior reform efforts, these foci are not often based on empirical research and promising practices (Jacobs et al., 2021; Samayeen et al., 2020). Instead, these calls for action are often driven by passionate voices of the community, sometimes following misguided and uniformed rhetoric, where slogans like "defund the police," "reimagine policing," or "abolish law enforcement," are used to spearhead changes. If the public, politicians, and police administrators want to "reimagine the police" by reforming the institution, such reforms should be firmly based on strong scholarly evidence about what works.

Probably the most disheartening aspect of the attempts to reform police organizations around the world is best summarized by Alpert and Mclean: "The more things change, the more they stay the same…" (2021). Although Alpert and Mclean's work (2021) focuses on the Australian police forces, the events across the United States in 2020 clearly demonstrate that the situation in American policing is analogous to that in Australia. Over a century-long story of independent police commissions in New York City provides further evidence of cycles of misconduct and reform; since 1890s, there was a twenty-year cycle in which, upon the public revelations of police misconduct and the scandal that followed, an independent commission was formed to investigate the NYPD and propose ways in which it should be reformed (e.g., Lexow Committee, 1894; Curran Committee, 1913; Seabury Report, 1932; Helfand Investigation, 1955; Knapp Commission, 1972; Mollen Commission, 1994). About two decades later, another discovery of serious police misconduct surfaces, followed by a new scandal, a new commission, and a new set of reforms.

What we knew about police misconduct, both in terms of its scope and intensity, pales in comparison to the knowledge we are gaining now, with the release of various police disciplinary records, like those recently made available by the New York City Police Department (Southall, 2021). The nation's largest police department released partial disciplinary records dating back to 2014 in an online dashboard containing profiles of all 35,000 active police officers. Separately, officials posted redacted copies of more than 200 decisions by judges in administrative trials, going back to 2017. For forty-four years, a section of the civil rights law known as 50-A had prevented the public from seeing most disciplinary records. However, in the aftermath of George Floyd's death in Minneapolis in the spring of 2020, the public demands and the political landscape started to change.

Within weeks, the New York State Legislature repealed the 50-A statute and a federal appeals court rejected the last effort of a legal challenge from police unions, which argued that releasing the records would put officers in danger and harm their careers. This decision created unprecedented access to police disciplinary records. In the eyes of many police critics, this development was perceived as "proof" of the systemic nature of police misconduct. A myriad of "experts" expressing their views on how police profession needs to be reimagined emerge almost on a daily basis. Community organizers and activists, potential victims of police misconduct and their families, politicians from various levels of government, and many others appear to uphold the view that this change can be predicated upon the scope of the complaints rather than solid empirical research and best practices.

At the heart of the problem lies the code of silence, the police cultural norm that prohibits disclosure of fellow officers' misconduct to supervisors. Recent Associated Press-NORC Center for Public Affairs Research public opinion polls about police reforms (2020, 2021) revealed that the American public is strongly in favor of controlling the code of silence; over 80% of the respondents on both polls said that they strongly or somewhat favor that police officers be required to report peer misconduct. Although the code, based on loyalty and brotherhood, may have a positive effect because it serves to protect police officers from outside threats (e.g., Kleinig, 2001), this camaraderie and loyalty can also have detrimental consequences for controlling the behavior of police officers—especially misconduct (Christopher Commission, 1991; Mollen Commission, 1994; President's Commission on Law Enforcement and the Administration of Justice, 1967; Skolnick, 2002). The Mollen Commission (1994) identified the code of silence as a pervasive element throughout the NYPD and pointed out that it "influences the vast majority of honest and corrupt officers alike." In fact, as Chin and Wells (1998, p. 237) argue, the code "prohibits disclosing perjury or other misconduct by fellow officers, or even testifying truthfully if the fact would implicate the conduct of a fellow officer." In fact, Chin and Wells view the code of silence as "evidence of bias and motive to lie" (1998, p. 233). The code of silence is not unique to the NYPD. To the contrary, the 2016 report by the Chicago Mayor's Police Accountability Task Force (2016, pp. 69–70) concluded that the code of silence "is institutionalized and reinforced by CPD rules and policies."

Moreover, the code of silence seems to be a pervasive part of police culture not only in the United States, but also across the world. While analyzing police-related scandals in Amsterdam, London, and New York, Punch (1985) discussed the role that the code of silence played in allowing police misconduct to exist. The Australian Fitzgerald Inquiry (1989, p. 216), which engaged in a systematic investigation of police and political corruption in Queensland and resulted in numerous prosecutions and convictions of top-ranked police officers, detected the code of silence among the Queensland police officers as well. The Fitzgerald Inquiry (1989, p. 216) connected the strong code of silence with the low level of police integrity: "[t]he unwritten police code is an integral element of police culture and has been a critical factor in the deterioration of the Police Force." Shortly after the Fitzgerald Inquiry, the Wood Royal Commission (1997) was tasked to investigate the existence and extent of police corruption within the New South Wales Police. The Commission faced an extensive code of silence, demonstrated through explicit detectives offering testimony at the hearings that directly conflicted with the undercover recordings of their misdeeds. In the report, the Wood Royal Commission (1997, p. 108) described the code as a serious impediment to investigating police misconduct.

The death of George Floyd in the spring of 2020 (Samayeen et al., 2020) and the subsequent 2021 conviction of Derek Chauvin, a former police officer from the Minneapolis Police Department, for Floyd's murder pointed to a small crack in the "blue wall of silence." In particular, many officers from Derek Chauvin's own department, including the Chief, testified that the tactics Chauvin used to subdue Mr. Floyd were inappropriate and inconsistent with training and policy (Sanchez et al., 2021). This was a very visible and rare moment in the history of police (dis) loyalty and solidarity.

The main goal of this book is to provide empirical research on and policy recommendations about the code of silence and police misconduct. We first assess the extent of the code of silence in a police organization and then, based on the findings, recommend changes that would lead toward the creation of an environment less tolerant of, and conducive for, police misconduct. We present an empirical case study that can provide a potential template for what needs to be done. Building upon over two decades of dissemination of a similar instrument in dozens of departments around the United States and in over 30 different countries (e.g., Kutnjak Ivković, 2015; Kutnjak Ivković & Haberfeld, 2019), we posit that the first step in creating change needs to the assessment and proper analysis of the attitudes of police officers in a given department, paired with the analyses of the ways in which the organization itself addresses police misconduct. The importance of this book lies in the empirical knowledge grounded in a case-study analysis that identifies the contours of the organizational subcultures that need to be addressed if transformational change is to be realized. If these recommendations are properly implemented, things might not "stay the same."

The Code of Silence

The code of silence, the informal prohibition of reporting misconduct by fellow police officers, is also called the "blue curtain" (Goldstein, 1970), "blue code" (Skolnick, 2002), and "blue wall of silence" (Bittner, 1970; Westley, 1970). Regardless of the term used, this concept refers to the informal cultural rule prohibiting police officers from blowing the whistle on the misconduct committed by fellow police officers. When Bernard Cawley, a former NYPD police officer, testified before the Mollen Commission entrusted to investigate allegations of police corruption in New York, he described the code of silence simply as "Cops don't tell on cops" (Mollen Commission, 1994, p. 53). The Christopher Commission, established after the beating of Rodney King and entrusted to investigate the use of excessive force and racism in the Los Angeles Police Department (1991), reported that the code of silence was described by an LAPD police officer as "a non-written rule that you do not roll over, tell on your partner" (Christopher Commission, 1991, p. 168).

Police subculture and its key element, the code of silence, have been a subject of steady inquiry for decades. As Crank (2014) points out, various subcultural themes of morality, solidarity, and fear influence individual behaviors of police officers. The beginnings of the scholarly approach to studying the code of silence in the United States date back more than 50 years. When Westley asked police officers in one of the first studies of police culture whether they would report a fellow police officer who stole money from a person arrested for drunkenness, the overwhelming majority of the officers—about three-quarters—reported that they would not, thus suggesting that "illegal action is preferable to breaking the secrecy of the group" (Westley, 1970, p. 113). More recent studies (e.g., Trautman, 2000; Weisburd & Greenspan, 2000) demonstrate that the code of silence is still strong. In a 2000 study by the U.S. National Institute of Ethics (Trautman, 2000, p. 1), 79 percent of the recruits nationwide agreed with the statement that the code of silence "exists and is fairly common across the nation." In a national study of more than 900 police officers from 121 police agencies, Weisburd and Greenspan (2000, p. 3) found that, although over 80% of the police officers said that they did not accept the code "as an essential part of the mutual trust necessary to good policing," the majority of the surveyed police officers agreed that it is not unusual for police officers to keep silent about misconduct by fellow officers, thus confirming the existence of the code of silence in police culture. At the same time, Weisburd and Greenspan's study (2000) demonstrated that the failure to abide by these cultural rules would probably result in informal negative consequences as most of the respondents agreed that police officers who decided to report misconduct would be given a cold shoulder from fellow officers for doing so. However, despite its seeming prevalence, the contours and the extent of the code may vary across police agencies, requiring careful assessment and measurement.

The research on the code of silence was jumpstarted when Klockars and Kutnjak Ivković (2004) proposed that the control of the code is an integral part of building of a police agency of integrity. They developed the theory of police integrity and the associated methodological approach for studying it. We now outline this theoretical and methodological approach because it is a foundation of the case study we present in the book.

The Code of Silence and the Theory of Police Integrity

The code of silence is also closely tied to the theory of police integrity (Klockars & Kutnjak Ivković, 2004). Based on the early work by Herman Goldstein about the organizational nature of police corruption (1970) and decades of empirical research on police misconduct, Klockars and Kutnjak Ivković (2004) developed the theory of police integrity that incorporates the code of silence as one of its four crucial dimensions. The theory of police integrity proposes that the level of police integrity in a police agency is closely tied to what the organization does, thus emphasizing the organizational nature of the theory. Police integrity is defined as "the normative inclination among police to resist temptations to abuse the rights and privileges of their occupation" (Klockars et al., 2006).

The first dimension of the theory establishes the importance of the police agency's organizational rules and the way they are established by the police administration, how they are communicated to the police officers, the degree to which police officers understand and support them, and the consistency with which they are enforced (e.g., Klockars & Kutnjak Ivković, 2004; Klockars et al., 2000, 2006; Kutnjak Ivković, 2015). A police agency of high integrity is viewed as a police agency in which the official rules contain detailed prohibitions of police misconduct, in which police officers are familiar with the official rules and support them, and in which official rules are consistently enforced for violations of these rules (Kutnjak Ivković, 2015).

The second dimension of the theory of police integrity emphasizes various techniques of controlling police misconduct (Klockars & Kutnjak Ivković, 2004; Klockars et al., 2000, 2006; Kutnjak Ivković, 2015). These control mechanisms could be reactive, such as internal investigations of police misconduct and imposition of discipline on police officers found to be in violation of the official rules, as well as proactive, such as police training on ethics and the use of early warning systems. A police agency of high integrity is expected to be a police agency that actively and consistently uses both proactive and reactive mechanisms to control police misconduct in the police agency (Kutnjak Ivković, 2015).

The third dimension of the theory of police integrity emphasizes the role of the code of silence and the police agency's ability to control it (Klockars & Kutnjak Ivković, 2004; Klockars et al., 2000, 2006; Kutnjak Ivković, 2015). While the code of silence develops in virtually every police agency as a consequence of the agency's paramilitary organization (Klockars et al., 2006), factors that differentiate police agencies of high integrity from police agencies of low integrity are how extensive the code is and what is protected by the code. In a police agency of high integrity, the code of silence is not strong, and it does not protect serious forms of police misconduct (Kutnjak Ivković, 2015). On the other hand, in police agencies of low integrity, the code of silence is strong, and it protects even the most serious forms of police misconduct.

The fourth dimension of the theory explores the connection between the society at large and the level of police integrity in the police agency (Klockars & Kutnjak Ivković, 2004; Klockars et al., 2000, 2006; Kutnjak Ivković, 2015). The authors argue that legal, political, economic, and societal conditions outside the police agency affect the level of police integrity within the police agency. Societies at large could enact the laws prohibiting misconduct by governmental employees, enforce these rules, and establish external agencies in charge of controlling misconduct, as well as develop cultural norms intolerant of misconduct of their public employees. Police agencies operating in such an environment will be more likely to have higher levels of police integrity as well.

Thus, the theory of police integrity reaffirms the importance of controlling the code of silence in police agencies as one of the tools critical to establishing a high level of integrity within police agencies. For scholars, policy-makers, and police executives interested in measuring the nature and strength of the code of silence, as well as the level of police integrity in general, Klockars and colleagues (1997, 2004, 2006) have developed a methodological approach that allows an empirical assessment. Because it is based on the measurement of fact and opinion, it is much less likely to be faced with resistance from police administrators and police officers alike than previous approaches that bluntly asked about the police officers' engagement in misconduct.

Measuring the Code of Silence

Because the theory assumes that police integrity is perceived as a belief, rather than the actual behavior (Klockars et al., 2006), it is easier to measure both police integrity in general and the code of silence in specific than if the focus were on actual police misconduct. The basic idea of this methodological approach is to develop a questionnaire that contains hypothetical scenarios describing examples of police misconduct and ask respondents questions directly measuring theoretical dimensions.

The first questionnaire, called the police corruption questionnaire, was created in the mid-1990s. It contains 11 scenarios, most of which described examples of police corruption (Klockars & Kutnjak Ivković, 2004; Klockars et al., 1997, 2000). It was based on Roebuck and Barker's typology of police corruption (1974). Because police integrity includes resistance to temptations of various sources and not only the for-gain variety (Klockars et al., 1997, 2000), the second version of the questionnaire—the police integrity questionnaire—contained a range of forms of police misconduct, including police corruption, use of excessive force, and falsification of the official report (Klockars et al., 2006). To allow for retesting, the same five scenarios were kept in both versions of the questionnaire.

The third version of the questionnaire—the basis of this book—expands the study of police integrity by incorporating not only scenarios describing police corruption and the use of excessive force, but also scenarios describing organizational deviance and interpersonal deviance (Kutnjak Ivković et al., 2019). There are three scenarios within each group, ranging in their seriousness from the least serious case of police misconduct to the most serious case of police misconduct within each group (Table 1.1). Scenarios addressing police corruption and the use of excessive force have originally been developed by Klockars et al. (2006) as a part of the police integrity questionnaire. Scenarios addressing organizational deviance and interpersonal deviance have been developed by Kutnjak Ivković et al. (2019).

Table 1.1 Scenarios

	Scenario Description
Police corruption	
Least serious	**Scenario 1:** A police officer is frequently seen in a neighborhood. Local merchants and restaurant owners regularly show their appreciation for his attention by giving him gifts of food and liquor and other items of small value.
Medium seriousness	**Scenario 4:** A police officer is scheduled to work during coming holidays. The supervisor offers to give him these days off, if he agrees to run some personal errands for the supervisor. Evaluate the SUPERVISOR'S behavior.
Most serious	**Scenario 2:** A police officer discovers a burglary of an appliance store. The display cases are smashed and many items have obviously been taken. While searching the store, he takes an expensive watch and slips it into his pocket. He reports that the watch, worth about a week's pay, has been stolen during the burglary.
Use of excessive force	
Least serious	**Scenario 5:** A police officer stops a motorist for speeding. As the officer approaches the vehicle, the driver yells, "what the hell are you stopping me for?" the officer replies, "because today is 'arrest an asshole day.'"
Medium seriousness	**Scenario 7:** A police sergeant, without intervening, watches officers under his supervision repeatedly strike and kick a man arrested for child abuse. The man has previous child abuse arrests. Evaluate the SERGEANT'S behavior.
Most serious	**Scenario 3:** An officer, who was severely beaten by a person resisting arrest, has just returned to duty. On patrol, the officer approaches a person standing in a dimly lit alley. Suddenly, the person throws a gym bag at the officer and begins to run away. The officer fatally shoots the person, striking him in the back. It was later determined that the person was unarmed.
Organizational deviance	
Least serious	**Scenario 8:** An officer is passed over for a day off on new Year's eve despite a promise from the supervisor. As a result, the officer could incur a financial loss for a nonrefundable family vacation. The police officer decides to call in sick for the new year Eve's shift and takes the trip.
Medium seriousness	**Scenario 6:** At 2 A.M. a police officer, who is on duty, is driving his patrol car on a deserted road. He sees a vehicle that has been driven off the road and is stuck in a ditch. He approaches the vehicle and observes that the driver is not hurt but is obviously intoxicated. He also finds that the driver is a police officer. Instead of reporting this accident and offense he transports the driver to his home.
Most serious	**Scenario 11:** Several days in a row, a police officer stays overtime to finish the paperwork. While filling out the forms requesting his overtime pay, he reports working one hour longer each day than he had actually worked.
Interpersonal deviance	
Least serious	**Scenario 12:** An officer is scheduled to attend a leadership training offered only to select members of the agency. After a disagreement with a supervisor, the officer is no longer on the list of officers scheduled to attend the training. The officer starts spreading a rumor that the supervisor's daughter is dating a drug addict. Evaluate the behavior of the officer.

(continued)

Table 1.1 (continued)

	Scenario Description
Medium seriousness	**Scenario 9:** Before the shift begins, several police officers gather in the police station to chat. After a few minutes, a male officer starts to taunt the female officers about their suitability for the job and makes jokes about their "other skills." evaluate the behavior of the male officer.
Most serious	**Scenario 10:** A traffic light is broken and a police officer is sent to direct traffic an hour prior to the end of his shift. He is assured by the supervisor that he is going to be relieved by officer Jones within 1 hour. After four hours, the light is fixed. The officer gets back to the station and upon spotting officer Jones yells: "Why the fuck didn't you show up to relieve me?"

After the respondents have read each scenario, they were asked the same seven questions. Three questions measured the first dimension of the theory of police integrity, that is, the role of the organizational rules, as they ask the respondents to evaluate how serious they view each of these behaviors, to estimate how serious they think that most police officers in their agency would evaluate these behaviors, and indicate whether these behaviors violate the official rules. The second dimension of the theory, focusing on the control mechanism, is measured through two questions in the questionnaire. The first question asks the respondents to state what they think that the appropriate discipline is for such behaviors and to predict what discipline they think that their police agency would mete out for such behaviors. Finally, the third dimension of the theory, tapping into the strength of the code of silence, was measured through two questions. The first question asked the respondents whether they would report such behavior to the supervisors and the second related question asked them to predict whether most police officers in their agency would report as well.

This third version of the questionnaire also contains questions that have previously not been included in the police integrity questionnaire. In particular, it measures organizational justice and police self-legitimacy. These concepts could potentially influence the level of police integrity within a police agency. The inclusion of these additional questions in the questionnaire opens the possibility to assess their importance in the shaping of the police agency's integrity. In the subsequent chapters, we explore these concepts in more detail and test the degree to which they are tied to police integrity.

Police Officer Sample

In December of 2018/January of 2019, the questionnaire was distributed online to police officers in a medium-size municipal police agency in the United States. Because of the conditions of our agreement with the police administration, we have to protect the confidentiality of the police agency and are limited in the extent of the information we may provide about the police agency and its officers. The police

Table 1.2 Sample demographic characteristics

Length of service	Frequency	Percent	Education	Frequency	Percent
Below 3 years	19	12.9%	High-school degree	31	20.3%
3–10 years	30	20.2%	Associate's degree	31	20.3%
10–20 years	47	31.8%	Bachelor's degree	66	44.6%
Over 20 years	52	35.1%	Master's degree or professional degree	21	14.1%
Gender					
Male	129	87.2%			
Female	19	12.8%			
Assignment					
Patrol	73	49.6%			
Detectives/investigations	35	23.7%			
Special operations, community policing	9	6.1%			
Administrative	26	17.6%			
Other	5	3.0%			
Supervisory role					
No	102	68.9%			
Yes	46	31.1%			

agency, a municipal police agency with between 250 and 500 sworn officers, serves a Southern urban community of 50,000 to 250,000 people, mostly composed of White residents.

Our sample of 148 respondents consists of experienced police officers; two-thirds of police officers in the sample have been police officers for at least 10 years (Table 1.2). They are also mostly male police officers (87%) and non-supervisors (69%; Table 1.2). They are primarily assigned to patrol (50%) and investigation (24%; Table 1.2). In terms of their education, our sample consists of educated police officers with about 60% having either a bachelor's degree or a master's/professional degree (Table 1.2).

Overview of the Book

The policing profession is under a great deal of scrutiny and criticism. Given the decentralized nature of the police profession in the United States, and the level of current unrest that generates outbursts of violent behaviors toward and against police officers, regardless of their actual involvement in perceived or actual misconduct, it is critical to address these grievances from an empirically informed perspective. Nearly a quarter of a century ago, Klockars and colleges (1997) launched a study of police integrity that focused on, among other factors, the source, scope, and prevalence of the code of silence. The code of silence was found in over 30 police departments throughout the United States (Klockars et al., 1997). Although its

Overview of the Book

scope and prevalence differed from one department to another, its existence was found to be empirically undeniable.

In the follow-up studies (Datzer et al., 2019; Donner et al., 2016, 2018, 2020; Ekenvall, 2003; Hickman et al., 2016; Kremer, 2000; Klockars et al., 2004, 2006; Kutnjak Ivković & Haberfeld, 2015; Kutnjak Ivković et al., 2018; Kutnjak Ivković & Klockars, 1998, 2000; Kutnjak Ivković et al., 2000, 2019, 2020; Kutnjak Ivković & Shelley, 2008, 2010; Kutnjak Ivković & Sauerman, 2011, 2012, 2013; Lim & Sloan, 2016; Long et al., 2013; Marche, 2009; Maskály et al., 2019; Micucci & Gomme, 2005; Pagon & Lobnikar, 2000, 2004; Porter & Prenzler, 2016; Schafer & Martinelli, 2008; Tasdoven & Kaya, 2014; Van Droogenbroeck et al., 2019; Westmarland, 2006; Westmarland & Rowe, 2018; Wu et al., 2018), researchers tied the code of silence and the explanations for its existence to a number of police officers' individual traits and, even more importantly, to organizational traits of their respective police departments. This book builds upon this body of research and ties the current state of affairs, based on our case study, to the individual factors and organizational factors that influence the code of silence prevalent in the twenty-first century.

This book addresses the need to update our knowledge about the prevalence of the code of silence. It focuses on the empirical findings linked to the creation of the theory of police integrity and tests the importance of traditional measures of police integrity. In addition, it explores the effect of perceptions of self-legitimacy from the individual and organizational standpoints. It also links police integrity with the police officers' perceptions of organizational justice and fair treatment by their supervisors. Finally, the book offers some insights for the path forward that are empirically, rather than emotionally driven.

Chapter 2 nests the code of silence within the discussion of police integrity. It starts by presenting an in-depth overview of the extant literature using the police integrity theory and the methodology developed by Klockars et al. (2004, 2006). Based on the data from one mid-sized police department in the United States, the chapter empirically examines the extent of the code of silence across 12 different scenarios depicting lapses in police integrity, including police corruption, use of excessive force, interpersonal deviance, and organizational deviance. It also explores the strength of respondents' perceptions of organizational factors and demographic factors predicting adherence to the code of silence.

Chapter 3 expands the traditional police integrity approach by looking at the effect of disciplinary fairness on the code of silence. Based on the theoretical model by Klockars and Kutnjak Ivković (1998), the chapter tests three potential theoretical approaches hypothesizing the nature of the relationship between the respondents' willingness to report misconduct and the evaluations of disciplinary fairness, namely the simple deterrence model, the simple justice model, and the discipline indifference model. The analyses in the chapter explore the effect of the perceptions of disciplinary fairness on the police officers' adherence to the code of silence while controlling for the traditional police integrity correlates.

Chapter 4 focuses on how the police officers' willingness to report is shaped by their perceptions of organizational justice. The notion of organizational justice has been a key factor driving the relationship between the employees and their organizations. A review of the extant literature indicates that police officers who believe that they receive fair treatment by their supervisors have higher levels of productivity, job satisfaction, and commitment to their organizations. The chapter builds on this body of literature by examining how perceptions of organizational justice relate to the adherence to the code of silence, while controlling for traditional police integrity variables.

Chapter 5 expands the police integrity approach by linking the police officers' willingness to adhere to the code of silence and their perspectives of their own legitimacy as police officers. Research suggests that a police officer's perception of self-legitimacy may influence how they interpret, evaluate, and respond to various situations. Hence, an emerging body of extant research suggests that the concept of self-legitimacy plays an important role in various outcomes associated with police officer attitudes and behaviors. The analyses in this chapter contribute to this body of literature by looking at the potential role that self-legitimacy may play in explaining why police officers decide to adhere to the code of silence.

Chapter 6 discusses the findings of a case study of a mid-size U.S. police agency in the context of extant research and elaborates on the lessons learned from our study. Based on an empirical study of the contours of the code of silence across behaviors that violate tenets of police integrity, including police corruption, use of excessive force, interpersonal deviance, and organizational deviance, the chapter illustrates the interconnectedness between the code of silence and the police agency's organizational and cultural perspectives. The study emphasizes the role that the police officers' cultural and organizational attitudes play in their willingness to adhere to the code of silence, from their perceptions of how willing other police officers are to report misconduct and the severity of the disciplinary threat that their police agency is making to their perceptions of self-legitimacy and organizational justice.

References

Alpert, G. P., McLean, K., & Wolfe, S. (2017). Consent decrees: An approach to police accountability and reform. *Police Quarterly, 20*(3), 239–249. https://doi.org/10.1177/1098611117709591

Alpert, G. P., & McLean, K. (2021). The more things change, the more they stay the same: The Queensland Police Service as a model for sustainable policing reform. *International Journal of Comparative and Applied Criminal Justice*. https://doi.org/10.1080/01924036.2021.1899004

Associated Press-NORC Center for Public Affairs Research. (2020). *Widespread desire for policing and criminal justice reform*. Available at https://apnorc.org/projects/widespread-desire-for-policing-and-criminal-justice-reform/

Associated Press-NORC Center for Public Affairs Research. (2021). *George Floyd's death: One year later*. Available at https://apnorc.org/projects/george-floyds-death-one-year-later/

Bayley, D., & Perito, R. (2011). Police corruption: What past scandals teach about current challenges. The United States Institute of Peace.

Bittner, E. (1970). *The functions of the police in modern society: A review of background factors, current practices, and possible role models*. National Institute of Mental Health, Center for Studies of Crime and Delinquency.

Chin, G. J., & Wells, S. C. (1998). The 'Blue Wall of Silence' as evidence of bias and motive to lie: A new approach to police perjury. *University of Pittsburgh Law Review, 59*(2), 233–300.

References

[Christopher Commission]. Independent Commission on the Los Angeles Police Department. (1991). *Report of the independent commission on the Los Angeles Police Department*. Author.

Cohen, G., & Taylor, R. W. (2014). Wilson, OW. *The Encyclopedia of Criminology and Criminal Justice*, 1–5.

Crank, J. P. (2014). *Understanding police culture*. Routledge.

[Curran Committee] Special Committee of the Board of Aldermen of the City of New York Appointed August 5, 1912 to Investigate the Police Department. (1913). *Report of the special committee of the Board of Aldermen of the City of New York Appointed August 5, 1912 to Investigate the Police Department*. Reprinted in Chin, G. J (Ed.)., New York City police corruption investigation commissions, 1984–1994. William S. Hein.

Datzer, D., Kutnjak Ivković, S., Mujanović, E., & Morgan, S. (2019). A complex relation between the code of silence and education. In S. Kutnjak Ivković & M. Haberfeld (Eds.), *Exploring police integrity: Novel approaches to police integrity theory and methodology*. Springer.

Donner, C., Maskaly, J., & Fridell, L. (2016). Social bonds and police misconduct: An examination of social control theory and its relationship to workplace deviance among police supervisors. *Policing: An International Journal of Police Strategies & Management, 39*(2), 416–431.

Donner, C. M., Maskaly, J., & Thompson, K. N. (2018). Self-control and the police code of silence: Examining the unwillingness to report fellow officers' misbehavior among a multi-agency sample of police recruits. *Journal of Criminal Justice, 56*, 11–19.

Donner, C. M., Maskaly, J., Popovich, N., & Thompson, K. N. (2020). Exploring the relationship between effective parenting, self-control, and adherence to the police code of silence. *Deviant Behavior, 41*(2), 137–159.

Ekenvall, B. (2003). Police attitudes toward fellow officers' misconduct: The Swedish case and a comparison with the USA and Croatia. *Journal of Scandinavian Studies in Criminology and Crime Prevention, 3*(2), 210–232.

[Fitzgerald Inquiry] Commission of Inquiry into Possible Illegal Activities and Associated Police Misconduct (1989). *Report of a Commission of inquiry pursuant to orders in council*. Author.

Fulton-Babicke, H. (2018). "I Can't Breathe": Eric Garner and in/out-group rhetorics. *Rhetoric Review, 37*(4), 434–446.

Goldsmith, A. (2005). Police reform and the problem of trust. *Theoretical Criminology, 9*(4), 443–470.

Goldstein, H. (1970). *Police corruption: A perspective on its nature and control*. Police Foundation.

[Helfand Investigation] District Attorney of Kings County. (1955). *Report of special investigation by the district attorney of Kings County, and the December 1949 grand jury*. Reprinted in Chin, G. J (Ed.), New York City police corruption investigation commissions, 1984–1994. William S. Hein.

Hickman, M. J., Powell, Z. A., Piquero, A. R., & Greene, J. (2016). Exploring the viability of an attitudes toward ethical behavior scale in understanding police integrity outcomes. *Policing: An International Journal of Police Strategies & Management, 39*(2), 319–337.

Jacobs, L. A., Kim, M. E., Whitfield, D. L., Gartner, R. E., Panichelli, M., Kattari, S. K., & Mountz, S. E. (2021). Defund the police: Moving towards an anti-carceral social work. *Journal of Progressive Human Services, 32*(1), 37–62.

Kappeler, V. E., Sluder, R. D., & Alpert, G. P. (1998). *Forces of deviance: Understanding the dark side of policing* (Vol. 2). Waveland Press.

Kleinig, J. (2001). The blue wall of silence. *The Journal of Applied Philosophy, 15*(1), 1–23.

Klockars, C. B., & Kutnjak Ivković, S. (2004). Measuring police integrity. In M. J. Hickman, A. R. Piquero, & J. R. Greene (Eds.), *Police integrity and ethics* (pp. 1.1–1.20). Wadsworth Publishing.

Klockars, C. B., Kutnjak Ivković, S., Harver, W. E., & Haberfeld, M. R. (1997). *The measurement of police integrity*. Final report submitted to the U.S. Department of Justice, Office of Justice Programs, National Institute of Justice.

Klockars, C. B., Kutnjak Ivković, S., Harver, W. E., & Haberfeld, M. R. (2000). *The measurement of police integrity, NIJ research in brief*. National Institute of Justice.

Klockars, C. B., Kutnjak Ivković, S., & Haberfeld, M. R. (Eds.). (2004). *Contours of police integrity*. Sage.

Klockars, C. B., Kutnjak Ivković, S., & Haberfeld, M. R. (2006). *Enhancing police integrity*. Springer Academic Publisher.

Knapp Commission. (1972). *Report of the commission to investigate allegations of police corruption and the city's anti-corruption procedures*. George Braziller.

Kremer, F. (2000). Comparing supervisor and line officer opinions about the code of silence: The case of Hungary. In M. Pagon (Ed.), *Policing in Central and Eastern Europe: Ethics, integrity, and human rights* (pp. 211–219). College of Police and Security Studies.

Kutnjak Ivković, S. (2015). Studying police integrity. In S. Kutnjak Ivković & M. Haberfeld (Eds.), *Police integrity across the World*. Springer.

Kutnjak Ivković, S., & Haberfeld, M. R. (Eds.). (2015). *Measuring police integrity across the World*. Springer Academic Publisher.

Kutnjak Ivković, S., & Haberfeld, M. R. (Eds.). (2019). *Exploring police integrity*. Springer Academic Publisher.

Kutnjak Ivković, S., Haberfeld, M. R., Cajner Mraović, I., Prpić, M., Hamm, J. A., & Wolfe, S. (2019). Seriousness of police (mis)behavior and organizational justice. In S. Kutnjak Ivković & M. Haberfeld (Eds.), *Exploring police integrity: Novel approaches to police integrity theory and methodology*. Springer.

Kutnjak Ivković, S., Haberfeld, M., & Peacock, R. (2018). Decoding the code of silence. *Criminal Justice Policy Review, 29*(2), 172–189.

Kutnjak Ivković, S., & Klockars, C. B. (1998). The code of silence and the Croatian police. In M. Pagon (Ed.), *Policing in Central and Eastern Europe: Organizational, managerial, and human resource aspects* (pp. 329–347). Ljubljana, Slovenia College of Police and Security Studies.

Kutnjak Ivković, S., & Klockars, C. B. (2000). Comparing police supervisor and line officer opinions about the code of silence: The case of Croatia. In M. Pagon (Ed.), *Policing in Central and Eastern Europe: Ethics, integrity, and human rights* (pp. 183–195). College of Police and Security Studies.

Kutnjak Ivković, S., Klockars, C. B., Lobnikar, B., & Pagon, M. (2000). Police integrity and the code of silence: A case of the Slovenian police force. In G. Mesko (Ed.), *Corruption in Central and Eastern Europe at the turn of millennium* (pp. 85–102). College of Police and Security Studies.

Kutnjak Ivković, S., Morgan, S. J., Cajner Mraović, I., & Borovec, K. (2020). Does the police code of silence vary with police assignment? An empirical exploration of the relation between the code and assignment. *Police Problems and Practices, 21*(2), 101–116.

Kutnjak Ivković, S., & Sauerman, A. (2011). Measuring the code of silence among the South African police: Findings from a SAPS supervisor survey. In C. Gould & G. Newham (Eds.), *Toward a coherent strategy for crime reduction in South Africa beyond 2010* (pp. 74–87). Institute for Security Studies.

Kutnjak Ivković, S., & Sauerman, A. (2012). The code of silence: Revisiting South African police integrity. *South African Crime Quarterly, 40*(June), 15–24.

Kutnjak Ivković, S., & Sauerman, A. (2013). Curtailing the code of silence among the South African police. *Policing: An International Journal of Police Strategies and Management, 36*(1), 175–198.

Kutnjak Ivković, S., & Shelley, T. O. (2008). The police code of silence and different paths toward democratic policing. *Policing and Society, 18*(4), 445–473.

Kutnjak Ivković, S., & Shelley, T. O. (2010). The code of silence and disciplinary fairness: A comparison of Czech police supervisor and line officer views. *Policing: An International Journal of Police Strategies and Management, 33*(3), 548–574.

[Lexow Committee] Special Committee Appointed to Investigate the Police Department of the City of New York. (1894). *Report of the special committee appointed to investigate Police Department of the City of New York*. Reprinted in Chin, G. J (Ed.), New York City Police corruption investigation commissions, 1984–1994. William S. Hein.

References

Lim, H., & Sloan, J. J. (2016). Police officer integrity: A partial replication and extension. *Policing: An International Journal of Police Strategies & Management, 39*(2), 284–301.

Long, M., Cross, J. E., Shelley, T. O., & Kutnjak Ivković, S. (2013). The normative order of reporting police misconduct: Examining the roles of offense seriousness, legitimacy, and fairness. *Social Psychology Quarterly, 76*(3), 242–267.

Marche, G. E. (2009). Integrity, culture, and scale: An empirical test of the big bad police agency. *Crime, Law, and Social Change, 51*, 463–486.

Maskály, J., Donner, C. M., & Chen, T. (2019). Improving the measurement of police integrity: An application of LTM to the Klockars et al. (1997) scales. In S. Kutnjak Ivković & M. Haberfeld (Eds.), *Exploring Police integrity*. Springer.

Micucci, A. J., & Gomme, I. M. (2005). American police and subcultural support for the use of excessive force. *Journal of Criminal Justice, 33*, 487–500.

[Mollen Commission] New York City Commission to Investigate Allegations of Police Corruption and the Anti-Corruption Procedures of the Police Department. (1994). *Commission report*. Author.

Pagon, M., & Lobnikar, B. (2000). Comparing supervisor and line officer opinions about the code of silence: The case of Slovenia. In M. Pagon (Ed.), *Policing in Central and Eastern Europe: Ethics, integrity, and human rights* (pp. 197–209). College of Police and Security Studies.

Pagon, M., & Lobnikar, B. (2004). Police integrity in Slovenia. In C. B. Klockars, S. Kutnjak Ivković, & M. R. Haberfeld (Eds.), *The contours of police integrity* (pp. 212–231). Sage.

Police Accountability Task Force. (2016). *Recommendations for reform: Restoring trust between the Chicago police and the communities they serve: Report*. Available at https://chicagopatf.org/wp-content/uploads/2016/04/PATF_Final_Report_4_13_16-1.pdf

Porter, L. E., & Prenzler, T. (2016). The code of silence and ethical perceptions: Exploring police officer unwillingness to report misconduct. *Policing: An International Journal of Police Strategies & Management, 39*(2), 370–386.

Punch, M. (1985). *Conduct unbecoming: The social construction of police deviance and control*. Tavistock.

Punch, M. (2000). Police corruption and its prevention. *European Journal on Criminal Policy and Research, 8*(3), 301–324.

Punch, M. (2009). *Police corruption: Deviance, accountability and reform in policing*. Routledge.

President's Commission on Law Enforcement and the Administration of Justice. (1967). *The challenge of crime in a free society*. United States Government Printing Office.

President's Task Force on 21st Century Policing. (2015). *Final report of the President's task force on 21st century policing*. Office of Community Oriented Policing Services.

Ray, R., Brown, M., Fraistat, N., & Summers, E. (2017). Ferguson and the death of Michael Brown on Twitter:# BlackLivesMatter,# TCOT, and the evolution of collective identities. *Ethnic and Racial Studies, 40*(11), 1797–1813.

Rhodes, D. J., Robinson, D. L., Archibald, P. C., & Van Sluytman, L. (2019). A decade's tale: Consent decrees and police use of disproportionate excessive force with communities of color. *Advances in Social Work, 19*(1), 217–238.

Roebuck, J. B., & Barker, T. (1974). A typology of police corruption. *Social Problems, 21*, 423–437.

Samayeen, N., Wong, A., & McCarthy, C. (2020). Space to breathe: George Floyd, BLM plaza and the monumentalization of divided American urban landscapes. *Educational Philosophy and Theory*. https://doi.org/10.1080/00131857.2020.1795980

Sanchez, R., Carrega, C, & Ellis, N. T. (2021). *The lessons of this moment. 'The testimony by police brass at Derek Chauvin's trial is unprecedented.'* Available at https://www.cnn.com/2021/04/10/us/derek-chauvin-george-floyd-trial-testimony/index.html

Schafer, J. A., & Martinelli, T. J. (2008). First-line supervisor's perceptions of police integrity. *Policing: An International Journal of Police Strategies and Management, 31*(2), 306–323.

[Seabury Report] Seabury, S. (1932). Final report of Samuel Seabury, referee, *in the matter of the investigation of the magistrates' courts in the first judicial department and the magistrates thereof, and of attorneys-at-law practicing in said courts*. [Reprinted in Chin, G. J (Ed.)., New York City police corruption investigation commissions, 1984–1994. William S. Hein].

Skolnick, J. (2002). Corruption and the blue code of silence. *Police Practice and Research, 3*(1), 7–19.

Southall, A. (2021). N.Y.P.D. releases secret misconduct records after repeal of shield law. *The New York Times*. Available at https://www.nytimes.com/2021/03/08/nyregion/nypd-discipline-records.html on 24 Mar 2021.

Tasdoven, H., & Kaya, M. (2014). The impact of ethical leadership on police officers' code of silence and integrity: Results from the Turkish National police. *International Journal of Public Administration, 37*, 529–541.

Trautman, N. (2000). *Police code of silence facts revealed*. In International Association of the Chiefs of Police, Annual conference. Available at http://www.aele.org/loscode2000.html

Van Droogenbroeck, F., Spruyt, B., Kutnjak Ivković, S., & Haberfeld, M. R. (2019). The effects of ethics training on police integrity. In S. Kutnjak Ivković & M. Haberfeld (Eds.), *Exploring police integrity: Novel approaches to police integrity theory and methodology*. Springer.

Walker, S. (2012). Institutionalizing police accountability reforms: The problem of making police reforms endure. *Saint Louis University Public Law Review, 32*(1), 57–92.

Weisburd, D., & Greenspan, R. (2000). *Police attitudes toward abuse of authority: Findings from a national study*. Office of Justice Programs.

Westmarland, L. (2006). Police ethics and integrity: Breaking the blue code of silence. *Policing and Society, 15*(2), 145–165.

Westley, W. (1970). Violence and the Police: A Sociological Study of Law, Custom and Morality. MIT Press.

Westmarland, L., & Rowe, M. (2018). Police ethics and integrity: Can a new code overturn the blue code? *Policing and Society, 28*(7), 854–870.

[Wood Royal Commission] Royal Commission into the New South Wales police service. (1997). *Final report*. The Government of the State of New South Wales.

Wu, G., Makin, D. A., Li, Y., Boateng, F. D., & Abess, G. (2018). Police integrity in China. *Policing: An International Journal, 41*(5), 563–577.

Open Access This chapter is licensed under the terms of the Creative Commons Attribution 4.0 International License (http://creativecommons.org/licenses/by/4.0/), which permits use, sharing, adaptation, distribution and reproduction in any medium or format, as long as you give appropriate credit to the original author(s) and the source, provide a link to the Creative Commons license and indicate if changes were made.

The images or other third party material in this chapter are included in the chapter's Creative Commons license, unless indicated otherwise in a credit line to the material. If material is not included in the chapter's Creative Commons license and your intended use is not permitted by statutory regulation or exceeds the permitted use, you will need to obtain permission directly from the copyright holder.

Chapter 2
The Code of Silence and the Theory of Police Integrity

Abstract This chapter nests the code of silence within the discussion of police integrity. It starts by presenting an overview of the tenets of police integrity theory and the methodology developed by Klockars CB, Kutnjak Ivković S, Haberfeld MR (2004a) The contours of police integrity. In Klockars CB, Kutnjak Ivković S, Haberfeld M R (eds). The contours of police integrity. Sage, Thousand Oaks, p 1–18.; Klockars CB, Kutnjak Ivković S, Haberfeld MR (2004b) Police integrity in the United States of America. In Klockars CB, Kutnjak Ivković S, Haberfeld M R (eds). The contours of police integrity. Sage, Thousand Oaks, p 265–282. Based on the data from one mid-sized police department in the United States, the chapter examines the extent of the code of silence across 12 different scenarios depicting lapses in police integrity, including police corruption, use of excessive force, organizational deviance, and interpersonal deviance. Our findings show that the strength of the code of silence varies across scenarios and that it is negatively related to how serious misconduct is evaluated to be. The multivariate models indicate that the perceptions of organizational peer culture are the strongest factor affecting the respondents' own willingness to report. In addition, other factors based on the police integrity theory—seriousness of police misconduct, assessment that the behavior violates official rules, and severity of expected discipline—are all related to the respondents' expressed unwillingness to adhere to the code of silence.

Keywords Police · Code of silence · Police misconduct · Police integrity · Seriousness · Police culture · Discipline

Introduction

Both Westley (1970) and Bittner (1971) argued that, because police work is dangerous and the danger is unpredictable, police recruits are taught at the police academy and subsequently by their field training officers that they should rely on and trust only their fellow officers. Socialization into the police culture then implies that, if police recruits want to be trusted by their more experienced peers and receive support when they need it, they should participate in the code of silence and keep close to their chest any information about police misconduct committed by fellow police officers.

The first empirical studies of the code in the United States could be traced back to Westley's study of the police profession (1970). A substantial increase in scholarship exploring the code of silence started in the 1990s, upon revelations that the code of silence is present and is an obstacle in any serious police reform. At the time, the Mollen Commission (1994, p. 53) in New York reported that the code of silence was prevalent in the NYPD and described it as "the most significant barrier to effective corruption control." Similarly, the Wood Commission in Australia (Wood, 1997) argued that the code of silence is a serious obstacle to a reform of the New South Wales Police Service. This was also the time when Klockars and colleagues (Klockars et al., 1997, 2000; Klockars & Kutnjak Ivković, 2004) proposed the theory of police integrity and developed the accompanying methodology, facilitating empirical studies of the code of silence.

This chapter utilizes the police integrity theory and the related methodology to explore the contours of police integrity in one U.S. police agency. We analyze the degree to which the code in this agency protects various forms of police misconduct, including police corruption, use of excessive force, organizational deviance, and interpersonal deviance. In the process, we also compare not only across different forms of police misconduct, but also across different levels of misconduct severity within each form of misconduct. In the subsequent multivariate analyses, we test the effects of traditional police integrity correlates on the police officers' adherence to the code of silence. In particular, we explore the influence of organizational factors, such as severity of expected discipline, familiarity with official rules, and expectations of fellow police officers' estimated willingness to report misconduct, on the police officers' reluctance to report misconduct.

Studying the Code of Silence

Ever since Klockars and colleagues (Klockars & Kutnjak Ivković, 2004; Klockars et al., 2000, 2004a, b, 2006) proposed this novel way of studying police misconduct, scholars across the world have used it to measure police integrity in general and the code of silence in particular. Specifically, the police integrity theory and the related methodology (e.g., Klockars et al., 1997, 2006; Klockars & Kutnjak Ivković, 2004) have been used to measure empirically the extent of the code of silence in about 30 countries across the world (for an overview, see Kutnjak Ivković, 2015a; see also Klockars et al., 2004a, b; Kutnjak Ivković & Haberfeld, 2015a, b), spanning across continents (e.g., North America, Europe, Asia, Africa, Australia), legal traditions (e.g., civil-law tradition, common-law tradition, Islamic), and levels of economic development (e.g., developed countries, countries in transition).

A number of the countries included in the studies are established democracies, such as Australia (Porter et al., 2015), Austria (Edelbacher & Kutnjak Ivković, 2004), Belgium (Van Droogenbroeck et al., 2019), Britain (Westmarland, 2004, 2005), Canada (Alain, 2004), Finland (Pounti et al., 2004), the Netherlands (Punch et al., 2004), Sweden (Torstensson Levander & Ekenvall, 2004), and the United States (e.g., Klockars et al., 1997, 2004b; Klockars & Kutnjak Ivković, 2004; Kutnjak Ivković et al., 2015). Extant research also included studies from countries in transition, such as Armenia (Khechumyan & Kutnjak Ivković, 2015; Kutnjak Ivković & Khechumyan, 2014), Bosnia and Herzegovina (Datzer et al., 2019; Kutnjak Ivković & Shelley, 2005, 2008), China (Wu & Makin, 2019), Croatia (Kutnjak Ivković & Klockars, 2004; Kutnjak Ivković, 2015b; Kutnjak Ivković et al., 2016), Estonia (Vallmüür, 2015, 2019), Poland (Haberfeld, 2004), Russia (Cheloukhine et al., 2015), Serbia (Peacock et al., 2020), Slovenia (Lobnikar & Meško, 2015), and South Africa (Sauerman & Kutnjak Ivković, 2015).

Although the strength of the code seemed to vary across countries or clusters of countries, at least some presence of the code of silence has been detected in every country covered by empirical studies to date. As Klockars and colleagues (Klockars et al., 2004a, p. 13) summarized the findings of their 14-country comparison, "[p]erhaps the most dramatic finding that emerges from examining the contours of integrity concerns the worldwide prevalence of the code of silence." To illustrate how diverse the contours of the code could be across the world, Klockars and colleagues (Klockars et al., 2004a, p. 17) further elaborated and emphasized that, in about one-third of the countries included in the study, "not a single incident out of the 11 incidents described in the survey would be very likely to be reported." On the other hand, in about one-third of the countries included in the study most, but not all of the incidents would not be protected by the code.

After they designed the police corruption questionnaire and collected the U.S. data, Klockars and colleagues (Klockars et al., 2000, p. 10) argued that the police corruption questionnaire addresses just one aspect of police integrity and that "the second generation of this survey" (i.e., the police integrity questionnaire) will provide coverage of other forms of police misconduct as well. This comparative 14-country study—utilizing the police corruption questionnaire—revealed substantial differences in the extent of the code of silence in terms of protecting different forms of police corruption (Klockars et al., 2004a). The subsequent 10-country study, based on the police integrity questionnaire (Kutnjak Ivković & Haberfeld, 2015b), provided further support to the claim that the extent of the code of silence varies greatly across the world and empirically confirmed that this conclusion holds not only for police corruption, but for other forms of police misconduct as well. However, no study to date of which we are aware has used the third version of the survey, one that incorporates an even wider range of scenarios—scenarios including examples of police corruption, use of excessive force, organizational deviance, and interpersonal deviance—to study the contours of the code of silence.

Correlates of the Code of Silence

Organizational Correlates

The theory of police integrity (Klockars et al., 1997, 2000, 2004a, b, 2006) is organizational in nature, stating that the police agency has a critical role in shaping the level of police integrity among its employees. To that end, as Klockars and Kutnjak Ivković (2004) were developing the theory and the related methodological approach, they introduced measures of these organizational components.

The first dimension of the theory focuses on the official rules and the way in which they are made by the administration, communicated to the police officers, and supported by them (Klockars et al., 2000, 2004a, b, 2006). The specific questions measuring this first dimension of the theory focus on the police officers' perceptions of misconduct seriousness and their familiarity with the official rules. Starting with the first survey conducted using this theoretical and methodological approach (Klockars et al., 2000), studies have consistently shown that the extent of the code of silence and the police officers' *own evaluations of misconduct seriousness* are strongly and negatively related (Cheloukhine et al., 2015; Haberfeld, 2004; Hickman et al., 2016; Khechumyan & Kutnjak Ivković, 2015; Klockars et al., 1997, 2004a, b, 2006; Kutnjak Ivković et al., 2013, 2018; Kutnjak Ivković & Khechymian, 2013; Kutnjak Ivković, Peacock, & Haberfeld, 2016; Kutnjak Ivković & Sauerman, 2013; Kutnjak Ivković, Haberfeld, Cajner Mraović, et al., 2019; Lobnikar & Meško, 2015; Long et al., 2013; Lim & Sloan, 2016; Maskály et al., 2019; Pagon & Lobnikar, 2000; Peacock et al., 2020; Porter & Prenzler, 2016; Vallmüür, 2015; Westmarland, 2006; Wu & Makin, 2019). This was the case not only within each country studied, but also across countries (e.g., Andreescu et al., 2012; Huberts et al., 2003; Klockars et al., 2004a; Kutnjak Ivković & Haberfeld, 2015a, b; Pagon et al., 2000). The most recent comparative study (Kutnjak Ivković & Haberfeld, 2015b) showed that the examples of police misconduct evaluated as the least serious, such as the acceptance of gratuities and a verbal abuse of citizens, are more likely to be protected by the code of silence than the examples of police misconduct evaluated as the most serious, such as stealing from a crime scene and abusing deadly force.

Evaluations of whether the example of police misconduct *violates official rules* constitute another measure of the first dimension of police integrity. The relationship between the police officers' familiarity with official rules and their willingness to stick to the code of silence has not been explored as frequently. However, the results show that familiarity with official rules is not such a strong predictor (e.g., Kutnjak Ivković et al., 2018; Peacock et al., 2020; Van Droogenbroeck et al., 2019). In a U.S. study exploring the effects of familiarity with official rules on the code of silence (Kutnjak Ivković et al., 2018), familiarity with official rules was significant in about one-half of the scenarios, but the effects disappeared in multivariate models in which other organizational variables have been included. Similarly, in a study of Belgian police officers, Van Droogenbroeck et al. (2019) discovered that familiarity with official rules was completely mediated through the perceived willingness to report by fellow police officers.

The second dimension of the theory focuses on the control mechanisms (Klockars et al., 2000, 2004a, b, 2006). Questions about the *appropriate discipline* and *expected discipline* (i.e., the discipline respondents anticipate that the police agency would mete out) measure this dimension (Klockars et al., 2000, 2004a, b, 2006). The severity of the expected discipline seems to be negatively related to the strength of the code of silence (e.g., Kutnjak Ivković et al., 2018; Kutnjak Ivković, Haberfeld, Cajner Mraović, et al., 2019; Kutnjak Ivković & Shelley, 2008; Lim & Sloan, 2016; Peacock et al., 2020; Wolfe & Piquero, 2011).

The third dimension of the theory focuses on the code of silence. The related methodology not only incorporates a question measuring the code of silence, but also contains a question measuring police officers' views about their peers' adherence to the code of silence. Specifically, the question measures perceptions about the *most police officers' willingness to report misconduct*. In extant literature, this measure was viewed as the measure of organizational culture within the police agency (e.g., Porter & Prezler, 2019), a deviant climate within the police organization (e.g., Lim & Sloan, 2016), and endorsement of peers (Long et al., 2013). Extant research uniformly shows that in multivariate models the estimates of peers' willingness to report are the most consistent and the strongest predictor of the respondents' own expressed willingness to report (Hickman et al., 2016; Kutnjak Ivković et al., 2018; Kutnjak Ivković et al., 2019; Lim & Sloan, 2016; Long et al., 2013; Peacock et al., 2020; Van Droogenbroeck et al., 2019).

Individual Correlates

The effect of several individual correlates has been previously tested in multivariate models of the code of silence. When included in the models, *supervisory status* is typically correlated with the respondents' own expressed willingness to report in most scenarios (Kutnjak Ivković et al., 2018; Kutnjak Ivković, Haberfeld, Cajner Mraović, et al., 2019; Long et al., 2013; Peacock et al., 2020), although some studies found it to be less significant (e.g., Lim & Sloan, 2016; Van Droogenbroeck et al., 2019). *Assignment* was also included in a few studies and yielded mixed results (e.g., Lim & Sloan, 2016; Long et al., 2013). In multivariate models, the *length of service* was typically found to be a non-significant predictor (Hickman et al., 2016; Kutnjak Ivković et al., 2018; Kutnjak Ivković, Haberfeld, Cajner Mraović, et al., 2019; Peacock et al., 2020; Van Droogenbroeck et al., 2019), occasionally displaying significance in some specific scenarios (e.g., Long et al., 2013).

These individual correlates also included demographic characteristics. Respondents' *gender* was rarely included in the multivariate models; when it was included, it was consistently shown to be unrelated to the respondents' willingness to report (Hickman et al., 2016; Van Droogenbroeck et al., 2019). Police officers' *education* is rarely explored in these models. Lim and Sloan (2016) found that it had a significant effect in only one out of the four types of scenarios. Similarly, Datzer et al. (2019) found that the educational level is not related to the police officers' expressed willingness to report, while the type of education (i.e., police-related education vs. general education) is.

This Chapter

Extant research on the code of silence has demonstrated that organizational variables are critical predictors, whereas individual characteristics are not such strong predictors of the police officers' expressed willingness to report. However, all prior studies of the code of silence have utilized the first police corruption questionnaire or the second police integrity questionnaire, but none have used the new version of the police integrity questionnaire that contains scenarios representing four types of police misconduct. This chapter follows in the footsteps of the traditional police integrity approach and incorporates traditional measures of police integrity in the analyses. At the same time, it expands the existing literature by exploring the effects of these critical variables in the scenarios describing not only police corruption and the use of excessive force, which have traditionally been used in the police integrity literature, but also in the scenarios of organizational deviance and interpersonal deviance, which have not been explored previously in the literature.

Methodology

Sample

In 2018/2019, we have surveyed police officers from a U.S. medium-size municipal police agency serving an urban community. The sample includes 148 police officers, both line officers and supervisors. For a detailed description of the characteristics of our sample and police agency, please see Chap. 1.

Measures

The analyses in this chapter are based on the results of the new version of the police integrity questionnaire (Kutnjak Ivković, Haberfeld, Cajner Mraović, et al., 2019) that includes scenarios dealing with police corruption, use of excessive force, organizational deviance, and interpersonal deviance. Upon reading the description of each scenario, the respondents were asked seven identical questions, targeting the respondents' perceptions of misconduct seriousness, their familiarity with the official rules, views about appropriate and expected discipline, and expressed willingness to report misconduct. For details, please see Chap. 1.

Dependent Variable

Our measure of the respondents' adherence to the code of silence—their *own willingness to report* misconduct—is based on the question asking the respondents to assess whether they would be willing to report the misconduct described in the scenario. The respondents could have selected an answer from a 5-point Likert-type scale, ranging from 1 = "definitely would not report" to 5 = "definitely would report." The responses were ultimately collapsed into two categories; values of 1 and 2 were coded as a 1 (i.e., adhere to the code of silence) and values of 3 through 5 were recoded as a 0 (i.e., not adhering to the code of silence). However, for the most severe scenarios depicting corruption (theft from a burglary scene) and excessive force (shooting a suspect in the back), we coded the variable differently: values 1 through 3 were coded as 1 (i.e., adhering to the code of silence) and values 4 and 5 were coded as 0 (i.e., not adhering to the code of silence).

The decision to code the answers in the most severe scenarios differently was made for three reasons. First, the bulk of the prior literature studying the code of silence has opted to collapse the variables in this manner. Thus, to make our results comparable with prior research we scaled our analyses the same way. Second, the distribution of willingness to report was definitively not uniform nor consistent across scenarios, which causes methodological problems for estimating multivariate effects. In other words, leaving the ordered version of the dependent variable almost ubiquitously violated the proportional odds assumption that is at the key of ordered logistic regression models (Long & Freese, 2014). Finally, when we looked at the distribution of responses, there was evidence of a Jenks break in the data, whereby there were two homogenous subgroups within the data that represented the respondents better than the initial five categories. This is not uncommon in Likert data, where participants frequently make a distinction without a difference (Davis, 1987).

Organizational Independent Variables

We have included several organizational variables in our models. The respondents were first asked to provide their *own evaluations of misconduct seriousness*. Possible answers to this question ranged on a 5-point Likert-type scale from 1 = "not at all serious" to 5 = "very serious."

The respondents were also asked whether they think that the behavior violates official rules. Possible answers to the question about *familiarity with the official rules* ranged on a 5-point scale from 1 = "definitely not" to 5 = "definitely yes."

There were also two questions about the discipline. The first question asked the respondents to share their views of the *appropriate discipline* for each example of police misconduct, while the next question asked them about their estimates of the *expected discipline*. In both questions, the respondents could have selected one of the six possible answers: 1 = "none" [no discipline], 2 = "verbal reprimand," 3 = "written reprimand," 4 = "period of suspension," 5 = "demotion in rank," 6 = "dismissal." For our multivariate models, we recoded the expected discipline into three categories: no discipline (1 = "no discipline" or 2 = "verbal reprimand"), some discipline (3 = "written reprimand," 4 = "suspension," and 5 = "demotion in rank"), and dismissal (6 = "dismissal").

We have also included another organizational variable that measures police officers' estimates of *most police officers' willingness to report*. The question asked the respondents to predict how likely most police officers in their police agency would be to report misconduct. The respondents could have selected one answer from a 5-point Likert-type scale, ranging from 1 = "definitely would not report" to 5 = "definitely would report."

Individual Independent Variables

We have included several variables measuring respondents' demographic characteristics into the questionnaire: their *length of service, gender, assignment, supervisory status*, and *education*.

Analytic Strategy

The analytic strategy for this chapter proceeds in two phases. In the first phase, we look at the contours of the code of silence across each of the scenarios. Specifically, we look at the distribution of the code of silence for each of the scenarios. In the second stage of the analyses, we build multivariate regression models that can predict the effects of the organizational independent variables on the code of silence, net of the other independent variables in the model.

Unlike larger datasets that can include many independent variables, we are limited by our sample size (N = 148). Logistic regression models require quite a bit of data to yield consistent and stable results. This is because the maximum likelihood estimator that is at the heart of the logistic regression makes assumptions about asymptotic normality, which is frequently violated without sufficient data (Ngunyi et al., 2014). While several recommendations have been developed for determining how many cases per variable are needed to include in a model, generally 20 observations per independent variable are required (Tabachnick & Fidell, 2019). In this case, our analyses would be limited to seven independent variables.

However, recent advancements in computational processing power allow scholars to make use of alternative estimation techniques in the family of machine learning, notably penalized regression models (Dezeure et al., 2015). These models add an extra constraint to the estimation equation such that the addition of more variables is more difficult (Friedman et al., 2010). We utilized LASSO regression models—one of the three primary forms of penalized regression (i.e., ridge regression, LASSO regression, and elastic net regression). The LASSO stands for the least absolute shrinkage and selection operator that estimates a penalty term (λ), which is a sum of all of the absolute coefficients in the model (Friedman et al., 2010). The benefit of the LASSO model is for the situations in which there is a high ratio of k (number of independent variables) to n (number of observations). Thus, the LASSO regression approach will allow us to use all of the information to develop the best subset of predictors to explain the dependent variable (Kammer et al., 2020). We use an extension of the LASSO model that allows for causal inferences to be made from the data, using the xpologit package in Stata 16.

At all stages of the multivariate analyses, we include all the independent variables and control variables that could be associated with a person's willingness to report misconduct. Given the design of the questionnaire, which seeks to promote honest reporting among officers by minimizing the risk that they could be identified through their survey responses, we have a limited number of control variables to select from. Specifically, we include *gender* ("female" vs. "male"), *assignment* ("patrol officers" vs. "other assignments"), *length of employment*, *education* (as a 4-level ordinal variable from high school, associate's degree, bachelor's degree, or master's degree or higher), and *supervisory status* ("yes" vs. "no"). The LASSO estimator will consider whether all variables in the model, independent and control, bring additional explanatory power to the model. In the tables below, there are no parameter estimates for these control variables as they do not yield additional explanatory power beyond the independent variables because they increase the value of the penalty term, λ.

Results

Contours of the Code of Silence

The respondents' expressed willingness to report misconduct varies greatly across the scenarios (Table 2.1), suggesting that the code of silence does not protect all misconduct equally. On the one hand, the respondents were least likely to say that they would protect a theft from a burglary scene, shooting the suspect in the back, and a supervisory failure to stop the beating (Ranks 1 to 3 in Table 2.1). The percent of the respondents who would protect such misconduct in silence is less than 20% and, for the two scenarios, actually well below 10% (Adhering to the Code of Silence in Table 2.1). On the other hand, the respondents were most likely to say that they would not report a colleague who yelled at co-workers, falsely reported being sick, and accepted gifts (Ranks 10–12 in Table 2.1). Over two-thirds of the respondents said that they would cover up such behaviors (Adhering to the Code of Silence in Table 2.1). The respondents' willingness to report misconduct is closely

Table 2.1 Contours of the code of silence

	1-Definitely would not report	2	3	4	5-Definitely would report	Adhering to code of silence (sum of 1–3)[a]	Rank code	Mean seriousness	Rank Ser.
Corruption									
Accepting gifts	30.8%	19.9%	14.4%	17.8%	17.1%	65.1%	10	3.20	10
Theft from burglary scene	1.6%	0.8%	2.7%	6.9%	88.0%	5.1%	1	4.99	1
Doing supervisor errands	10.3%	15.2%	24.4%	14.1%	36.0%	49.8%	6	4.04	6
Excessive use of force									
Shooting suspect in back	1.1%	0.8%	3.8%	5.1%	89.2%	5.7%	2	4.91	2
Verbally abusing citizen	22.5%	16.9%	17.5%	20.1%	23.0%	56.9%	8	3.48	9
Supervisor fails to stop beating	4.4%	5.9%	8.4%	25.3%	56.0%	18.7%	3	4.69	3
Organizational deviance									
Covering up DUI crash	15.1%	18.6%	17.9%	15.0%	33.4%	51.6%	7	3.74	7
False sick report	42.4%	10.8%	20.0%	8.9%	17.9%	73.2%	11	2.71	11
False overtime reporting	7.9%	13.3%	15.5%	21.9%	41.4%	36.8%	5	4.29	5
Interpersonal deviance									
Telling sexist jokes	8.9%	7.4%	16.4%	15.6%	51.8%	32.6%	4	4.40	4
Yelling at coworkers	52.0%	19.0%	14.6%	5.1%	9.4%	85.5%	12	2.15	12
False rumors about coworker	16.3%	13.5%	28.2%	17.9%	24.2%	58.0%	9	3.76	8

[a] Because there are so few respondents who selected an answer other than "5" for "theft from burglary scene" and "shooting suspect in back," the distribution for these two scenarios was very skewed and, for the purposes of multivariate analyses, we dichotomized the variables differently for these two scenarios (1–4 vs. 5) than we did for all other scenarios (1–3 vs. 4–5).

related to their perceptions of how serious the misconduct is (Table 2.1): there was a very strong correlation between the ranking of scenarios based on the respondents' willingness to report and the ranking of scenarios based on the respondents' assessments of scenario seriousness (Spearman's rho = .993, $p < .001$).

There is also a substantial variation in the respondents' expressed willingness to report within each type of misconduct. Within *police corruption*, stealing from a crime scene was expected to be much less protected by the code than accepting gratuities (Table 2.1). While about one-half or more police officers would protect the acceptance of gratuities (65%) and running errands for a supervisor (50%), only a small proportion of police officers would tolerate a theft from a crime scene in silence (5%). There is also a substantial variation within the three scenarios describing the *abuse of force*. In particular, the majority of the respondents would cover a police officer who verbally abused a citizen (57%), but only less than 20% would protect a supervisor who did not stop the beating and less than 10% would not report a fellow officer who abused deadly force (Table 2.1). Within scenarios describing *organizational deviance*, only a minority of the officers would protect false overtime reporting in silence (37%), while about one-half of the respondents (52%) would cover a fellow officer's DUI accident and the overwhelming majority (73%) would protect a fellow police officer who falsely reported sick. The variation existed in the scenarios of *interpersonal deviance* as well; a minority of the respondents (33%) would not report an officer who was telling sexist jokes, but the majority would not report an officer who was spreading false rumors in the agency (58%) or yelling at co-workers (86%).

The Effects of Police Integrity Measures on the Code of Silence

We next looked at the multivariate results from the LASSO models to explain what factors affect officers' adherence to the code of silence. To aid in the interpretation of the results, we group the results based on the type of misconduct (i.e., corruption, excessive force, organizational deviance, and interpersonal deviance).

Police Corruption

The results from all scenarios dealing with police corruption are generally consistent with prior police integrity literature (Table 2.2). To begin with, respondents who believe that other police officers are more likely to adhere to the code of silence are also more likely to say that they would adhere to the code themselves. However, this effect is not consistent in magnitude across all types of scenarios, whereby the effect of perceived others' adherence to the code is the weakest—yet still significant and rather large in magnitude—for receiving gifts and the strongest for supervisory corruption.

Likewise, we see that either a recognition that a particular act is a violation of policy (odds ratio (OR) = 0.42, $p < .001$) or an evaluation of an act as serious (OR = 0.36, $p < .001$) is negatively associated with the code of silence. The direction of the effects for these two variables is consistent for supervisory errands, but only significant for recognition that this act is a violation of policy (OR = 0.66, $p < .05$). We cannot estimate these parameters for the situation depicting the theft from a burglary scene because the act is almost universally noted as a violation of policy and something that is seen as very serious by our respondents. Yet, some officers report they will adhere to the code of silence even in this case (OR = 43.88, $p < .001$).

Table 2.2 The code of silence and police integrity theory estimates

	Corruption			Excessive force		
	Gifts	Theft from burglary	Supervisor errands	Shooting suspect in the back	Verbally abusing citizen	Failing to report beating
Others' code of silence	13.19***	43.88***	86.57***	172.72***	83.18***	135.02***
Violation of policy	0.42***	–	0.66*	0.07***	0.33***	1.18
Own perceptions of seriousness	0.36***	–	0.78	0.01***	0.31***	0.05***
No discipline[a]	2.55***	16.59***	2.07**	0.01***	1.98**	0.60
Dismissal[a]	1.37	1.09	2.85***	0.56	10.29***	3.17**
χ^2 (df)	378.5 (5)	150.81 (3)	409.32 (5)	102.26 (5)	305.67 (5)	300.88 (5)
	Organizational deviance			Interpersonal deviance		
	Covering up DUI crash	False sick report	False overtime reporting	Telling sexist jokes	Yelling at coworkers	Spreading false rumors about coworker
Others' code of silence	38.89***	92.15***	80.19***	56.56***	24.01***	48.33***
Violation of policy	0.75*	0.74*	2.45***	1.22	2.73***	0.37***
Own perceptions of seriousness	0.20***	0.12***	0.05***	0.28***	0.10***	0.71***
No discipline[a]	0.65	27.71***	1.38	3.08***	2.25**	2.40***
Dismissal[a]	0.83	0.25*	1.58	3.03	11.77	8.47*
χ^2 (df)	325.03 (5)	148.89 (5)	277.47 (5)	269.75 (5)	139.27 (5)	184.46 (5)

* $= p < .05$, ** $= p < .01$, *** $= p < .001$
– = parameters excluded due to collinearity
[a] Reference category is "intermediate discipline"

We also explored the effect of perceptions of discipline severity on the police officers' adherence to the code of silence. The results suggest that in all three corruption scenarios, compared to the officers who indicated that some intermediate discipline is expected, officers who expected no discipline were more likely to say that they would adhere to the code of silence, with the effect being most pronounced for the scenario depicting theft from a burglary scene (OR = 16.59, $p < .001$). This suggests that officers who expect no discipline are unlikely to come forward and report these sorts of behaviors. On the other hand, the respondents who expected dismissal were only significantly more likely to say that they would adhere to the code of silence in the case depicting supervisory corruption (OR = 2.85, $p < .001$).

Use of Excessive Force

Next, we look at the results for the scenarios depicting situations of *excessive force*, also presented in Table 2.2. Again, in all three scenarios, we see that the belief that others will adhere to the code of silence is a robust predictor of officers saying that they would personally adhere to the code of silence. Furthermore, the magnitude of this effect across all three excessive force scenarios is among the strongest effects for this variable across all scenarios in this chapter.

Additionally, in two of the scenarios we see that officers who acknowledge that these situations are a violation of department policy are less likely to say that they would adhere to the code of silence, except for the situation depicting the supervisor who failed to stop a beating, although this was not significant (OR = 1.18, $p > .05$). Universally, officers who think these sorts of situations are serious are less likely to say that they would adhere to the code of silence. The magnitude of the effect corresponds with the general rank seriousness of the events. In other words, the strongest effect of seriousness is seen in the situation involving the most serious conduct (i.e., shooting a suspect in the back; OR = 0.01, $p < .001$), followed by failing to report a beating (OR = 0.05, $p < .001$), and it is the lowest in magnitude for verbally abusing a citizen (OR = 0.31, $p < .001$).

Turning to the effect of discipline severity, the pattern of findings is complicated. Notably, compared to the police officers who expected some intermediate discipline, officers who expected no discipline seemed to have a lower likelihood of adhering to the code of silence for the scenario depicting the use of deadly force (OR = 0.01, $p < .001$), whereas they have a higher likelihood of adhering to the code of silence for the scenario depicting a verbal abuse of a citizen (OR = 1.98, $p < .01$). There was no significant effect for the scenario depicting the beating of a suspect (OR = 0.60, $p > .05$). Conversely, compared to the respondents who selected some intermediate discipline, the respondents who selected dismissal were more likely to say that they would adhere to the code of silence in the scenario with the verbal abuse of a citizen (OR = 10.29, $p < .001$) and in the scenario describing a failure to report a beating (OR = 3.17, $p < .01$).

Organizational Deviance

Next, we turn to the results for the scenarios depicting *organizational deviance* presented in Table 2.2. Across scenarios, consistent with prior research, feeling that others will adhere to the code of silence is a consistent, significant, and strong predictor that an officer will adhere to the code of silence in all three scenarios. Additionally, we see the familiar pattern that those officers who find the actions depicted in these scenarios as more serious are less likely to say that they would adhere to the code of silence. Recognizing the actions as a violation of departmental policy shows different effects depending on the scenario. For the scenarios of covering up the DUI crash of a fellow officer (OR = 0.75, $p < .05$) and false sick report (OR = 0.74, $p < .05$) the recognition that this is a policy violation decreases adherence to the code of silence. However, recognizing that filing a false overtime report is a violation of department policy is positively related to adhering to the code of silence (OR = 2.45, $p < .001$).

Unlike prior scenario types, there is only one scenario where the type of expected discipline exerts a significant effect. Notably, we see that, compared to the officers who expected some intermediate discipline, officers who expected no discipline (OR = 27.71, $p < .001$) were more likely to say that they would adhere to the code of silence in the scenario depicting the false sick report. Additionally, compared to the officers who expected some intermediate discipline, officers who expected dismissal were less likely to say that they would adhere to the code in case of an officer who falsely called in sick to work (OR = 0.25, $p < .05$). There are no significant, or even consistent, patterns of findings for the expected discipline variables in the other two organizational deviance scenarios.

Interpersonal Deviance

Finally, we look at the results from *interpersonal deviance*, shown in Table 2.2. We see the familiar pattern that the anticipated other officers' adherence to the code of silence is consistently, significantly, and positively related to their own willingness to adhere to the code of silence. We also see that officers who perceive these situations as serious are universally less likely to say that they would adhere to the code of silence. The effect for the variable recognizing the act as a violation of department policy does not yield consistent results: one scenario shows a negative effect (spreading false rumors about coworker, OR = 0.37, $p < .001$), one has a positive effect (yelling at coworkers, OR = 2.73, $p < .001$), and one has a null effect (telling sexist jokes, OR = 1.22, $p > .05$).

The results for discipline again present a complicated pattern of results. We see that, compared to the officers who expected some intermediate discipline, officers who expected no discipline were more likely to say that they would adhere to the code of silence in all three scenarios (Table 2.2). The same pattern of results is seen for dismissal compared to an intermediate discipline, although the effect is only statistically significant for the scenario depicting the spreading of false rumors about a coworker (OR = 8.47, $p < .05$).

Conclusion

Our results show that the code of silence exists among the police officers in the police agency we study. Such a finding should not be surprising, having in mind that the code of silence is a universal phenomenon that the police integrity research was able to document since the 1990s (e.g., Klockars et al., 2000, 2004a, b; Kutnjak Ivković & Haberfeld, 2015a, b, 2019). A more pressing question is how strong the code of silence is in the police agency included in our case study. Apart from two

Conclusion

scenarios describing blatant examples of not only police misconduct, but serious criminal conduct, at least 20% of police officers would protect in silence *all* other examples of police misconduct in our questionnaire. While this percent may not look high, it very vividly indicates that the code of silence is not only present, but also strong. Whereas this percentage may not seem overwhelming, one-fifth of a police agency could constitute a large number of police officers, and even a single officer's engagement in misconduct, particularly when it involves the abuse of deadly force and/or racism, may generate strong reactions, including riots, destructions, and a tremendous pushback against police legitimacy and integrity.

Our results show that the code of silence is not a flat prohibition of reporting and that the police officers' expressed willingness to report is strongly related to how serious they perceive misconduct to be: the more serious they evaluate the misconduct, the less likely they are to say that they would protect it by the code of silence. Although the new police integrity questionnaire has expanded the types of police misconduct included in the questionnaire, our results fit well with the already established line of research focusing primarily on police corruption and the use of excessive force, demonstrating the interconnectedness between the perceptions of seriousness and the expressed willingness to report misconduct (Cheloukhine et al., 2015; Haberfeld, 2004; Hickman et al., 2016; Khechumyan & Kutnjak Ivković, 2015; Klockars et al., 1997, 2004a, b, 2006; Kutnjak Ivković et al., 2013, 2018; Kutnjak Ivković & Khechymian, 2013; Kutnjak Ivković, Peacock, & Haberfeld, 2016; Kutnjak Ivković & Sauerman, 2013; Kutnjak Ivković, Haberfeld, Cajner Mraović, et al., 2019; Lobnikar & Meško, 2015; Long et al., 2013; Lim & Sloan, 2016; Maskály et al., 2019; Pagon & Lobnikar, 2000; Peacock et al., 2020; Porter & Prenzler, 2016; Vallmüür, 2015; Westmarland, 2006; Wu & Makin, 2019).

Perceptions of how other police officers would react—whether they would adhere to the code of silence or not—are one of the strongest and definitely most consistent predictors of the respondents' own determination to adhere to the code of silence. Our findings of an influential organizational culture are consistent with prior research about the code of silence that has demonstrated the close connection between our own anticipated behavior and the expected behavior of the peer group (Hickman et al., 2016; Kutnjak Ivković et al., 2018; Kutnjak Ivković, Haberfeld, Cajner Mraović, et al., 2019; Lim & Sloan, 2016; Long et al., 2013; Peacock et al., 2020; Van Droogenbroeck et al., 2019). Indeed, police officers feel that they are a part of the police culture and they seem dependent upon what they anticipate that their peers would do.

The effects of the expected discipline severity are uniform neither across all types of misconduct nor within each type of misconduct. On the one hand, in the scenarios describing police corruption and interpersonal deviance, expecting no discipline compared to some intermediate discipline increased the likelihood that officers would say that they adhere to the code of silence. On the other hand, such a relationship was not as prominent or even in the same direction for some of the scenarios describing the use of excessive force and organizational deviance.

Similarly, when we analyzed the effect of discipline severity within each type of misconduct, we found, for example, that, compared to intermediate discipline, dismissal was linked with higher adherence to the code of silence for the scenarios describing an instance of verbal abuse of a citizen and for the scenario describing a failure to report a beating, but not for the scenario describing the abuse of deadly force. These findings are particularly salient given the national conversation around the police use of force, especially deadly force. These results could represent a backlash to the enhanced scrutiny that police officers are currently experiencing. Also, it is troubling that disciplining this type of behavior more seriously could have deleterious effects on officers' willingness to report this type of misconduct.

While the severity of the expected discipline seems to be an important factor for the respondents' decision whether to adhere to the code of silence in a number of scenarios, our present analyses do not reveal how fair the respondents evaluated this expected discipline and, even more importantly for the purposes of our study, whether their perceptions of discipline fairness are related to their willingness to report. In the next chapter, we turn our attention to the issue of discipline fairness and its effect on the police officers' determination to adhere to the code of silence.

References

Alain, M. (2004). An exploratory study of Quebec's police officers' attitudes toward ethical dilemmas. In C. B. Klockars, S. Kutnjak Ivković, & M. R. Haberfeld (Eds.), *The contours of police integrity* (pp. 40–56). Sage.

Andreescu, V., Keeling, D., Vito, G. T., & Voinic, M. C. (2012). Romanian and American police officers' perceptions of professional integrity and ethical behavior. *Revista Română de Sociologie, XXIII*(3–4), 185–207.

Bittner, E. (1971). *The functions of the police in modern society*. U.S. Government Printing Office.

Cheloukhine, S., Kutnjak Ivković, S., Haq, Q., & Haberfeld, M. R. (2015). Police integrity in Russia. In S. Kutnjak Ivković & M. Haberfeld (Eds.), *Police integrity across the world*. Springer.

Datzer, D., Kutnjak Ivković, S., Mujanović, E., & Morgan, S. (2019). A complex relation between the code of silence and education. In S. Kutnjak Ivković & M. Haberfeld (Eds.), *Exploring police integrity: Novel approaches to police integrity theory and methodology*. Springer.

Davis, R. V. (1987). Scale construction. *Journal of Counseling Psychology, 34*(4), 481–489.

Dezeure, R., Buhlmann, P., Meier, L., & Meinshausen, N. (2015). High-dimensional inference: Confidence intervals, p-values and R-software. *Statistical Science, 30*(4), 533–558.

Edelbacher, M., & Kutnjak Ivković, S. (2004). Ethics and the police: Studying police integrity in Austria. In C. B. Klockars, S. Kutnjak Ivković, & M. R. Haberfeld (Eds.), *The contours of police integrity* (pp. 19–39). Sage Publications.

Friedman, J., Hastie, T., & Tibshirani, R. (2010). Regularization paths for generalized linear models via coordinate decent. *Journal of Statistical Software, 33*(1), 22.

Haberfeld, M. R. (2004). The heritage of police misconduct: The case of the polish police. In C. B. Klockars, S. Kutnjak Ivković, & M. R. Haberfeld (Eds.), *The contours of police integrity* (pp. 95–210). Sage Publications.

Hickman, M. J., Powell, Z. A., Piquero, A. R., & Greene, J. (2016). Exploring the viability of an attitudes toward ethical behavior scale in understanding police integrity outcomes. *Policing: An international journal of police strategies & management, 39*(2), 319–337.

Huberts, L., Lamboo, T., & Punch, M. (2003). Police integrity in the Netherlands and the United States: Awareness and alertness. *Police practice and research, 4*(3), 217–232.

References

Kammer, M., Dunkler, D., Michiels, S., & Heinze, G. (2020). Evaluating methods for Lasso selective inference in biomedical research by a comparative simulation study. *arXiv*. preprint arXiv:2005.07484.

Khechumyan, A., & Kutnjak Ivković, S. (2015). Police integrity in Armenia. In S. Kutnjak Ivković & M. Haberfeld (Eds.), *Police integrity across the world*. Springer.

Klockars, C. B., & Kutnjak Ivković, S. (2004). Measuring police integrity. In M. Hickman, A. R. Piquero, & J. R. Greene (Eds.), *Police integrity and ethics*. Wadsworth.

Klockars, C.B., Kutnjak Ivković, S., Harver, W. E., & Haberfeld, M.R.. (1997). *The measurement of police integrity*. Final Report Submitted to the U.S. Department of Justice, Office of Justice Programs, National Institute of Justice.

Klockars, C. B., Kutnjak Ivković, S., Harver, W. E., & Haberfeld, M. R. (2000). *The measurement of police integrity, NIJ research in brief*. National Institute of Justice.

Klockars, C. B., Kutnjak Ivković, S., & Haberfeld, M. R. (2004a). The contours of police integrity. In C. B. Klockars, S. Kutnjak Ivković, & M. R. Haberfeld (Eds.), *The contours of police integrity* (pp. 1–18). Sage Publications.

Klockars, C. B., Kutnjak Ivković, S., & Haberfeld, M. R. (2004b). Police integrity in the United States of America. In C. B. Klockars, S. Kutnjak Ivković, & M. R. Haberfeld (Eds.), *The contours of police integrity* (pp. 265–282). Sage Publications.

Klockars, C. B., Kutnjak Ivković, S., & Haberfeld, M. R. (2006). *Enhancing police integrity*. Springer.

Kutnjak Ivković, S., & Klockars, C. B. (2004). Police Integrity in Croatia. In Klockars, C. B., Kutnjak Ivković, S., & M. R. Haberfeld (Eds.). *The Contours of Police Integrity* (pp. 56–74). Thousand Oaks, CA: Sage Publications.

Kutnjak Ivković, S., & Khechumyan, A. (2013). The State of Police Integrity in Armenia: Findings from the Police Integrity Survey. *Policing: An International Journal of Police Strategies and Management, 36*(1), 70–90.

Kutnjak Ivković, S. (2015a). Studying police integrity. In S. Kutnjak Ivković & M. Haberfeld (Eds.), *Measuring police integrity across the world*. Springer.

Kutnjak Ivković, S. (2015b). Police integrity in Croatia. In S. Kutnjak Ivković & M. Haberfeld (Eds.), *Police integrity across the world*. Springer.

Kutnjak Ivković, S., & Haberfeld, M. R. (Eds.). (2015a). *Measuring police integrity across the world*. Springer.

Kutnjak Ivković, S., & Haberfeld, M. (2015b). A comparative perspective on police integrity. In S. Kutnjak Ivković & M. Haberfeld (Eds.), *Police integrity across the world*. Springer.

Kutnjak Ivković, S., & Khechumyan, A. (2014). Measuring police integrity among urban and rural police in Armenia: From local results to global implications. *International Journal of Comparative and Applied Criminal Justice, 38*(1), 39–61.

Kutnjak Ivković, S., & Sauerman, A. (2013). Curtailing the code of silence among the South African Police. *Policing: An International Journal of Police Strategies and Management, 36*(1), 175–198.

Kutnjak Ivković, S., & Shelley, T. O. (2005). The Bosnian police and police integrity: A continuing story. *European Journal of Criminology, 2*(4), 428–454.

Kutnjak Ivković, S., & Shelley, T. O. (2008). The police code of silence and different paths toward democratic policing. *Policing and Society, 18*(4), 445–473.

Kutnjak Ivković, S., & Shelley, T. O. (2010). The code of silence and disciplinary fairness: A comparison of Czech police supervisor and line officer views. *Policing: An International Journal of Police Strategies and Management, 33*(3), 548–574.

Kutnjak Ivković, S., Haberfeld, M., & Peacock, R. (2013). Rainless West: The integrity survey's role in agency accountability. *Police Quarterly, 16*(2), 148–176.

Kutnjak Ivković, S., Haberfeld, M., & Peacock, R. (2015). Police integrity in the United States. In S. Kutnjak Ivković & M. Haberfeld (Eds.), *Police integrity across the world*. Springer.

Kutnjak Ivković, S., Peacock, R., & Haberfeld, M. (2016). Does Discipline Fairness Matter for the Police Code of Silence? Answers from the U.S. Supervisors and Line Officers. *Policing: An International Journal of Police Strategies and Management, 39*(2), 354–369.

Kutnjak Ivković, S., & Haberfeld, M. R. (Eds.).(2019). *Exploring Police Integrity: Novel Approaches to Police Integrity Theory and Methodology.* New York: Springer.

Kutnjak Ivković, S., Cajner Mraović, I., & Borovec, K. (2016). An empirical test of the influence of society at large on police integrity in a centralized police system. *Policing: An International Journal of Police Strategies & Management, 39*(2), 302–318.

Kutnjak Ivković, S., Haberfeld, M., & Peacock, R. (2018). Decoding the code of silence. *Criminal Justice Policy Review, 29*(2), 172–189.

Kutnjak Ivković, S., Haberfeld, M. R., Cajner Mraović, I., Prpić, M., Hamm, J. A., & Wolfe, S. (2019). Seriousness of police (mis)behavior and organizational justice. In S. Kutnjak Ivković & M. Haberfeld (Eds.), *Exploring police integrity: Novel approaches to police integrity theory and methodology.* Springer.

Kutnjak Ivković, S., Haberfeld, M. R., & Peacock, R. (2019). Overlapping shades of blue: Exploring police officer, supervisor, and administrator cultures of police integrity. In S. Kutnjak Ivković & M. Haberfeld (Eds.), *Exploring police integrity: Novel approaches to police integrity theory and methodology.* Springer.

Lim, H., & Sloan, J. J. (2016). Police officer integrity: a partial replication and extension. *Policing: An International Journal of Police Strategies & Management, 39*(2), 284–301.

Lobnikar, B., & Meško, G. (2015). Police integrity in Slovenia. In S. Kutnjak Ivković & M. Haberfeld (Eds.), *Police integrity across the world.* Springer.

Long, J. S., & Freese, J. (2014). *Regression models for categorical dependent variables using stata* (3rd ed.). Stata Press.

Long, M., Cross, J. E., Shelley, T. O., & Kutnjak Ivković, S. (2013). The normative order of reporting police misconduct: Examining the roles of offense seriousness, legitimacy, and fairness. *Social Psychology Quarterly, 76*(3), 242–267.

Maskály, J., Donner, C. M., & Chen, T. (2019). Improving the measurement of police integrity: An application of LTM to the Klockars et al. (1997) scales. In S. Kutnjak Ivković & M. Haberfeld (Eds.), *Exploring police integrity.* Springer.

Mollen, M. (1994). *Anatomy of failure: A path for success, Mollen report.* Commissions to Investigate Allegations of Police Corruption and the Anti-Corruption Procedures of the New York Police Department.

Ngunyi, A., Mwita, P., & Odhiambo, R. (2014). On the Estimation and Properties of Logistic Regression Parameters. *IOSR Journal of Mathematics, 10,* 57–68.

Pagon, M., & Lobnikar, B. (2000). Comparing supervisor and line officer opinions about the code of silence: The case of Slovenia. In M. Pagon (Ed.), *Policing in Central and Eastern Europe: Ethics, integrity, and human rights* (pp. 197–209). College of Police and Security Studies.

Pagon, M., Kutnjak Ivković, S., & Lobnikar, B. (2000). Police integrity and attitudes toward police corruption: A comparison between the police and the public. In M. Pagon (Ed.), *Policing in central and eastern Europe: ethics, integrity, and human rights* (pp. 383–396). College of Police and Security Studies.

Peacock, R., Prpić, M., Kutnjak Ivković, S. Cajner Mraović, I., & Božović, V. (2020). Shades of blue: Exploring the code of silence in Croatia and Serbia. *International Journal of Comparative and Applied Criminal Justice.* Forthcoming. https://doi.org/10.1080/01924036.2020.1824872

Porter, L. E., & Prenzler, T. (2016). The code of silence and ethical perceptions: Exploring police officer unwillingness to report misconduct. *Policing: An International Journal of Police Strategies & Management, 39*(2), 370–386.

Porter, L. E., Prenzler, T., & Hine, K. (2015). Police integrity in Australia. In S. Kutnjak Ivković & M. Haberfeld (Eds.), *Measuring police integrity across the world.* Springer.

Porter, L., & Prenzler, T. (2019). Exploring Gender Differences In the Australian Context: Organizational and Cultural Dimensions of Ethical Attitudes. In Kutnjak Ivković, S. and

References

M. Haberfeld (Eds.), *Exploring Police Integrity: Novel Approaches to Police Integrity Theory and Methodology*. New York: Springer.

Pounti, A., Vuorinen, S., & Kutnjak Ivković, S. (2004). Sustaining police integrity in Finland. In C. B. Klockars, S. Kutnjak Ivković, & M. R. Haberfeld (Eds.), *The contours of police integrity* (pp. 95–115). Sage Publications.

Punch, M., Huberts, L. W. J. C., & Lamboo, M. E. D. (2004). Integrity, perceptions, and investigations in the Netherlands. In C. B. Klockars, S. Kutnjak Ivković, & M. R. Haberfeld (Eds.), *The contours of police integrity* (pp. 161–175). Sage Publications.

Sauerman, A., & Kutnjak Ivković, S. (2015). Police integrity in South Africa. In S. Kutnjak Ivković & M. Haberfeld (Eds.), *Police integrity across the world*. Springer.

Tabachnick, B. G., & Fidell, L. S. (2019). *Using multivariate statistics* (7th ed.). Pearson.

Torstensson Levander, M., & Ekenvall, B. (2004). Homogeneity in moral standards in Swedish police culture. In C. B. Klockars, S. Kutnjak Ivković, & M. R. Haberfeld (Eds.), *The contours of police integrity* (pp. 251–265). Sage Publications.

Vallmüür, B. (2015). Police Integrity in Estonia. In S. Kutnjak Ivković & M. Haberfeld (Eds.), *Police integrity across the world*. Springer.

Vallmüür, B. (2019). The contours of an organizational theory of green police integrity. In S. Kutnjak Ivković & M. Haberfeld (Eds.), *Exploring police integrity*. Springer.

Van Droogenbroeck, F., Spruyt, B., Kutnjak Ivković, S., & Haberfeld, M. R. (2019). The effects of ethics training on police integrity. In S. Kutnjak Ivković & M. Haberfeld (Eds.), *Exploring police integrity: Novel approaches to police integrity theory and methodology*. Springer.

Westley, W. (1970). *Violence and the police: A sociological study of law, custom, and morality*. MIT Press.

Westmarland, L. (2004). Policing integrity: Britain's thin blue line. In C. B. Klockars, S. Kutnjak Ivković, & M. R. Haberfeld (Eds.), *The contours of police integrity* (pp. 75–93). Sage Publications.

Westmarland, L. (2005). Police ethics and integrity: Breaking the blue code of silence. *Policing and Society, 15*(2), 145–165.

Westmarland, L. (2006). Police ethics and integrity: Breaking the blue code of silence. *Policing and Society, 15*(2), 145–165.

Wolfe, S. E., & Piquero, A. R. (2011). Organizational justice and police misconduct. *Criminal justice and behavior, 38*(4), 332–353.

Wood, J. (1997). *Royal commission into the New South Wales police service. Final Report, Vol. 1*. Government of the State of New South Wales.

Wu, G., & Makin, D. A. (2019). The quagmire that is an unwillingness to report: Situating the code of silence within the Chinese police context. *Criminal Justice and Behavior, 46*(4), 608–627.

Open Access This chapter is licensed under the terms of the Creative Commons Attribution 4.0 International License (http://creativecommons.org/licenses/by/4.0/), which permits use, sharing, adaptation, distribution and reproduction in any medium or format, as long as you give appropriate credit to the original author(s) and the source, provide a link to the Creative Commons license and indicate if changes were made.

The images or other third party material in this chapter are included in the chapter's Creative Commons license, unless indicated otherwise in a credit line to the material. If material is not included in the chapter's Creative Commons license and your intended use is not permitted by statutory regulation or exceeds the permitted use, you will need to obtain permission directly from the copyright holder.

Chapter 3
The Code of Silence and Disciplinary Fairness

Abstract This chapter expands the police integrity approach by focusing on the link between the evaluations of disciplinary fairness and the code of silence. Based on the writings by Klockars and Kutnjak Ivković (The code of silence and the Croatian police. In Pagon M (ed) Policing in central and Eastern Europe: organizational, managerial, and human resource aspects. College of Police and Security Studies, Ljubljana, Slovenia, 329–347, 1998), this chapter presents three potential theoretical approaches hypothesizing the relationship between police officers' willingness to report misconduct and disciplinary fairness. We rely on the data from one mid-sized police department in the United States to test the effects across 12 scenarios depicting police corruption, use of excessive force, interpersonal deviance, and organizational deviance. Our multivariate models show that perceptions of disciplinary fairness are independently related to the police officers' willingness to adhere to the code of silence. Discipline that is viewed as too harsh does not entice police officers to report; rather, in such cases, police officers are more likely to say that they would not report than police officers who evaluated discipline as fair. The effects are not as clear for the cases in which police officers evaluated discipline as too lenient.

Keywords Police · Code of silence · Police misconduct · Police integrity · Discipline · Dismissal · Fairness · Distributive fairness

Introduction

Empirical work in this book is grounded in the police integrity theory and the related methodology (Klockars & Kutnjak Ivković, 2004; Klockars et al., 1997, 2000, 2004, 2006). Since Klockars and colleagues (Klockars & Kutnjak Ivković, 2004; Klockars et al., 2000, 2004, 2006) proposed the theory of police integrity and designed an empirical way to measure integrity, many scholars across the world have relied on it to assess the level of police integrity in their national or local police agencies (Alain, 2004; Cheloukhine et al., 2015; Edelbacher & Kutnjak Ivković,

2004; Datzer et al., 2019; Haberfeld, 2004; Khechumyan & Kutnjak Ivković, 2015; Kutnjak Ivković et al., 2016a, Kutnjak Ivković & Khechumyan, 2014; Kutnjak Ivković & Shelley, 2005, 2008; Lobnikar & Meško, 2015; Peacock et al., 2020; Porter et al., 2015; Pounti et al., 2004; Punch et al., 2004; Sauerman & Kutnjak Ivković, 2015; Torstensson Levander & Ekenvall, 2004; Vallmüür, 2015, 2019; Van Droogenbroeck et al., 2019; Westmarland, 2004, 2006; Wu & Makin, 2019).

Although the key pillars of discipline fairness measurement have been incorporated in the early traditional police integrity approach (Klockars et al., 1997), it was the first extension of the work by Klockars and Kutnjak Ivković (Kutnjak Ivković & Klockars, 1998) in which the topic of disciplinary fairness was included in the police integrity discussions. In particular, Klockars and Kutnjak Ivković (Kutnjak Ivković & Klockars, 1998) hypothesized what the potential influence of the evaluations of disciplinary fairness should be on the police officers' willingness to report misconduct. Starting from the early writings by Klockars and colleagues (Kutnjak Ivković & Klockars, 1998; Klockars et al., 2000), the issue of disciplinary fairness has been included in police integrity research, albeit not to the same extent as more traditional measures of police integrity. A handful of subsequent studies that utilized this approach provided mixed results (e.g., Datzer et al., 2019, Kutnjak Ivković et al., 2016b; Kutnjak Ivković & Sauerman, 2013; Kutnjak Ivković & Shelley, 2005, 2007, 2010).

This chapter relies on the police integrity theory and the accompanying methodology to assess the relationship between the code of silence and the perceptions of discipline fairness. Following the approach developed by Klockars and Kutnjak Ivković (Kutnjak Ivković & Klockars, 1998), we empirically test the nature of the relationship along three proposed theoretical models. In the process, we also study this relationship not only across different forms of police misconduct, but also across different levels of misconduct severity within each form of misconduct. In the subsequent multivariate analyses, we test the effect of the perceptions of disciplinary fairness and traditional police integrity correlates on the police officers' adherence to the code of silence. In particular, while controlling for the influence of organizational factors (e.g., evaluations of misconduct seriousness, severity of expected discipline, familiarity with official rules, expectations of fellow police officers' estimated willingness to report misconduct), we assess the importance of the respondents' evaluations of disciplinary fairness for their reluctance to report misconduct.

Discipline Fairness and Police Integrity

Although the theory of police integrity (Klockars & Kutnjak Ivković, 2004; Klockars et al., 1997, 2000, 2004, 2006) does not directly link discipline fairness and police integrity (e.g., Klockars et al., 1997), a framework has been established for the exploration of the relationship between the respondents' expressed willingness to report and the perceptions of organizational distributive discipline fairness (Kutnjak Ivković & Klockars, 1998).

Theoretical Approaches

Klockars and Kutnjak Ivković (Kutnjak Ivković & Klockars, 1998) argued that the police officers' evaluations of discipline their police agency will mete out for a specific violation of the official rules should be related to their willingness to report misconduct. To test this relationship, they proposed three models in which the perceptions of disciplinary fairness could be related to the respondents' willingness to report misconduct (Kutnjak Ivković & Klockars, 1998; Fig. 3.1).

The first model—simplified deterrence—assumes that discipline harshness is the primary reason why police officers would be willing to report misconduct. It implies that the harsher the discipline, the more likely police officers are to report misconduct. Hence, the proportion of police officers willing to report misconduct would be the highest for the police officers who evaluated the expected discipline as too harsh and would be the lowest for the police officers who evaluated the expected discipline as too lenient. It is a simplified model because it takes into account only discipline severity but omits both its celerity and certainty (Kutnjak Ivković & Klockars, 1998).

The second model—discipline indifferent—simply assumes that there is no relationship between the police officers' willingness to report and their evaluations of

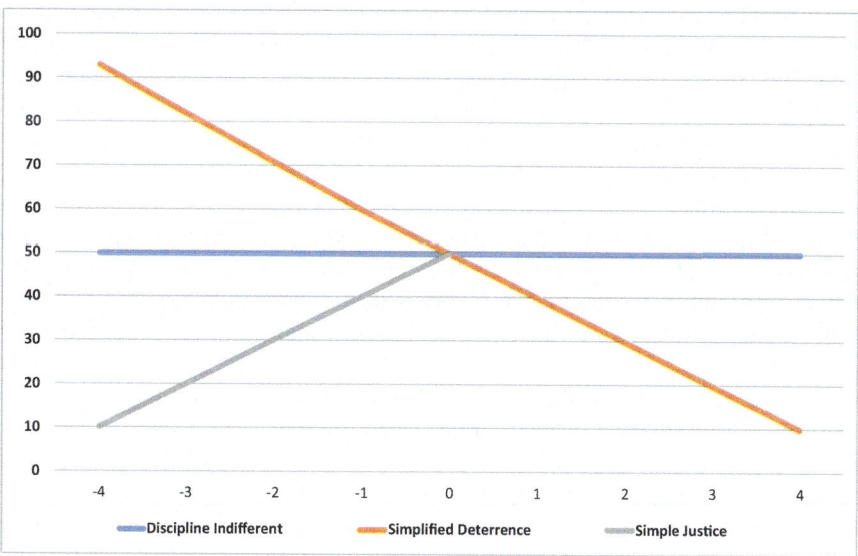

Fig. 3.1 Hypothetical effect of discipline fairness on willingness to report under three theoretical models

discipline fairness. Hence, the proportion of police officers adhering to the code of silence is the same, regardless of how fair they evaluated the expected discipline to be. Kutnjak Ivković and Klockars (1998) offered reasons that may explain this relationship. To begin with, although police officers may think that the discipline is harsh, this evaluation would have no effect on their willingness to report because they believe that the certainty of receiving any discipline from their police agency is rather low. Alternatively, the code may be so strong that any potential effects of discipline harshness would be lost on it.

The third model—simple justice—assumes that the police officers' primary motivation for reporting misconduct lies in the fact that they want to see misconduct disciplined justly or fairly (Kutnjak Ivković & Klockars, 1998). Hence, the percent of police officers willing to report misconduct would be higher among those evaluating the discipline as fair than among those who are evaluating the discipline as too harsh. However, the prediction for the right side of the graph is less clear; Kutnjak Ivković and Klockars (1998, p. 335) argue that, "[t]he motive of simple justice would offer no reason for increased reporting of misconduct under conditions of excessive leniency." It is quite possible that the relation could remain flat or become negative when discipline is evaluated as too lenient.

Empirical Measurement of Discipline Fairness

The empirical measures of discipline fairness are based on the second dimension of the theory of police integrity, which focuses on the police agency's control efforts and their influence on the level of police integrity in the police agency. Klockars and Kutnjak Ivković (2004) developed two questions tapping into this theoretical dimension. First, they asked the respondents to state what they think that the appropriate discipline is for the examples of misconduct described in the questionnaire. Second, they asked the respondents to predict what discipline their police agency would mete out for a police officer who engaged in such misconduct. Subtracting the expected discipline from the appropriate discipline determines how *fair* the respondent is evaluating the severity of the expected discipline. If the difference is zero, the respondent is evaluating the expected discipline as *fair*. On the one hand, if the difference is negative, the respondent evaluates the expected discipline as *too harsh*. Finally, if the difference is positive, the respondent evaluates the expected discipline as *too lenient*.

The difference between the answers to the questions about the appropriate and the expected discipline can range from −4 to +4 (Fig. 3.1). However, Kutnjak Ivković and Klockars (1998) pointed out that these are ordinal scales. Accordingly, instead of comparing the respondents' willingness to report for each numeric value, they condensed the respondents into three categories: (1) the respondents who evaluated the discipline as *too harsh* (values −4 to −1), (2) the respondents who evaluated the discipline as *fair* (value 0), and (3) the respondents who evaluated the discipline as *too lenient* (values +1 to +4). The studies that tested the relationship between the code of silence and perceptions of disciplinary fairness typically followed this classification.

Studying the Relationship Between the Code of Silence and Perceptions of Disciplinary Fairness

In their original paper, Kutnjak Ivković and Klockars (1998) reported that, compared to the respondents who evaluated the expected discipline as too harsh, the respondents who evaluated it as fair were much more willing to say that they would report misconduct. Hence, they found consistent evidence supporting the simple justice model. On the other hand, a comparison between the respondents who perceived the expected discipline as fair and those who evaluated it as too lenient yielded small differences, suggesting in most of the scenarios at best a modest and positive relationship between willingness to report and perceptions of fairness, a finding indicative of the simple justice model as well.

Several subsequent studies tested the model and reported mixed results. When they focused on the left side of the graph (comparing the expressed willingness to report by the respondents who perceived the expected discipline as too harsh with those who evaluated the expected discipline as fair), some of the studies from Bosnia and Herzegovina (Datzer et al., 2019), the Czech Republic (Kutnjak Ivković & Shelley, 2007, 2010), and the United States (Kutnjak Ivković et al., 2016b) provided support for the simple justice model. On the other hand, studies from South Africa (Kutnjak Ivković & Sauerman, 2013) and older studies from Bosnia and Herzegovina (Kutnjak Ivković & Shelley, 2005) provided evidence supporting the discipline indifferent model. In both countries, the code of silence was very strong at the time of the study, and it seems that perceptions of the expected discipline harshness at the time would have had no significant effect on the police officers' willingness to report.

When these police integrity studies focused on the right side of the graph (comparing the expressed willingness to report by the respondents who perceived the expected discipline as fair with those who evaluated the expected discipline as too lenient), the results were more uniform. Although occasionally some scenarios seem to fit the simple justice model or the simple deterrence model, in the overwhelming majority of the scenarios the model of discipline indifference works best (Datzer et al., 2019; Kutnjak Ivković & Klockars, 1998; Kutnjak Ivković et al., 2016b; Kutnjak Ivković & Sauerman, 2013; Kutnjak Ivković & Shelley, 2005, 2007, 2010). In other words, the percentage of the respondents willing to report misconduct does not depend on whether they evaluated the discipline as fair or too lenient. It seems that, on this side of the graph, discipline harshness does not matter as much as does its certainty.

This Chapter

This chapter expands the traditional police integrity approach toward the study of the code of silence by adding the measures of discipline fairness into the models. Extant research exploring the relationship between the respondents' willingness to report misconduct and their perceptions of disciplinary fairness has yielded mixed results. If perceptions of disciplinary fairness were found to be related to the code of silence, the relationship mostly appears to fit the simple justice model because police officers who evaluated the expected discipline as too harsh seem to be less likely to say that they would report than the respondents who evaluated the expected discipline as fair. On the other hand, if police officers perceived the expected discipline as too lenient, they seem to be as likely to say that they would report as police officers who evaluated the expected discipline as fair, thus typically fitting the no relationship, discipline indifferent model. This chapter utilizes the same approach in the study of the relationship between the code of silence and perceptions of disciplinary fairness. It expands the existing literature by exploring this relationship not only for the traditional police corruption and the use of excessive force scenarios, but also for the organizational deviance and interpersonal deviance scenarios. We first explore the nature of the bivariate relationship and then engage in multivariate models, in which this relationship is explored while controlling for the traditional police integrity measures.

Methodology

Sample

In 2018/2019, we have surveyed police officers from a medium-size municipal police agency in the United States. Our sample of 148 police officers comes from a municipal police agency that serves an urban community. For a detailed description of the characteristics of our sample and police agency, please see Chaps. 1 and 2.

Measures

The analyses in this chapter assess the effect of the respondents' perceptions of disciplinary fairness on their willingness to adhere to the code of silence. All measures are included in the new version of the police integrity questionnaire (Kutnjak Ivković et al., 2019) that includes scenarios dealing with police corruption, use of excessive force, organizational deviance, and interpersonal deviance. After they read the description of misconduct in each of the scenarios, the respondents answered seven questions. These questions asked them to evaluate examples of

Methodology   43

police misconduct and state how serious they evaluate the misconduct, whether they perceive that it violates official rules, what they think that the appropriate discipline should be, what discipline they think that their police agency would mete out, and how willing they would be to report the misconduct. For details, please see Chaps. 1 and 2.

Dependent Variable

Our measure of the respondents' adherence to the code of silence, based on their *own willingness to report* misconduct, is asking the respondents to assess whether they would be willing to report misconduct described in the scenario. The respondents could have selected an answer from a 5-point Likert-type scale, ranging from 1 = "definitely would not report" to 5 = "definitely would report." The responses were ultimately collapsed into two categories, with values of 1 and 2 recoded as 1 (i.e., adhere to the code of silence) and values of 3 through 5 recoded as 0. There are two exceptions to this rule. In particular, for the most severe scenarios depicting corruption (theft from a burglary scene) and excessive force (shooting a suspect in the back), we recoded 1 through 3 as 1 (i.e., adhering to the code of silence) and 4 and 5 as 0. For details, please see Chap. 2.

Organizational Independent Variables

We have included several organizational variables in our models. They include measures of the respondents' own evaluations of misconduct *seriousness*, their estimates of whether the misconduct described in the scenario *violates official rules*, their estimates of *appropriate* and *expected* discipline, and their estimates of *most police officers' willingness to report*. For a more detailed description, please see Chap. 2.

Disciplinary Fairness Independent Variables

The *discipline fairness* measure was obtained by deducting the respondents' answers to the question about the expected discipline from their answer to the question about the appropriate discipline. There are six possible answers to the questions about expected and appropriate discipline (1 = "none" [no discipline], 2 = "verbal reprimand," 3 = "written reprimand," 4 = "period of suspension," 5 = "demotion in rank," 6 = "dismissal"). Because there are six disciplinary options, the values of the variable measuring disciplinary fairness could range from −5 to +5. The value of 0 indicates that the respondents evaluated the expected discipline as fair (i.e., they selected the same disciplinary option as both the appropriate discipline and the expected discipline). Because we were interested in determining whether the discipline was seen as fair, too harsh, or too lenient, we recoded the values −5 to −1 as "discipline too harsh" and values 1 to 5 as "discipline too lenient." Thus, we created two indicator variables, "too harsh discipline" and "too lenient discipline," that were compared against those who thought the expected discipline was fair.

For all scenarios, between 58% (falsely calling in sick) and 85% (shooting suspect in the back) of the respondents evaluated the expected discipline as fair. Most officers who were identified as evaluating the discipline as either too harsh or too lenient were typically within two points from zero. In other words, very few officers felt as though there were going to be vast differences between the discipline one should receive and the discipline one would likely receive.

Individual Independent Variables

Several variables measured the respondents' demographic characteristics. They include the respondents' *length of service, gender, assignment, supervisory status*, and *education*. Because of the small sample size, we used these demographic characteristics as the control variables in our multivariate models. Please see Chap. 2 for details.

Analytic Strategy

The analytic strategy for this chapter proceeds in two phases. In the first phase, we examine the willingness to report misconduct based on the disciplinary fairness expected by the respondents. Note that we intentionally report *willingness to report*, capturing the logical complement of the code of silence, to facilitate integrating the results with prior literature. The second stage of the analyses incorporates the measures of disciplinary fairness into our multivariate models that explain adherence to the code of silence, net of other police integrity variables. Again, we group the results together by scenario type for ease of interpretation. We continue to use the LASSO models to generate the parameter estimates. For a more detailed description of this method, please see Chap. 2.

Results

The Effects of Discipline Fairness on the Code of Silence

We follow the analytical approach developed by Klockars and Kutnjak Ivković (Kutnjak Ivković & Klockars, 1998). Thus, we first focus on the relationship between the respondents' willingness to report and their perceptions of disciplinary

Results

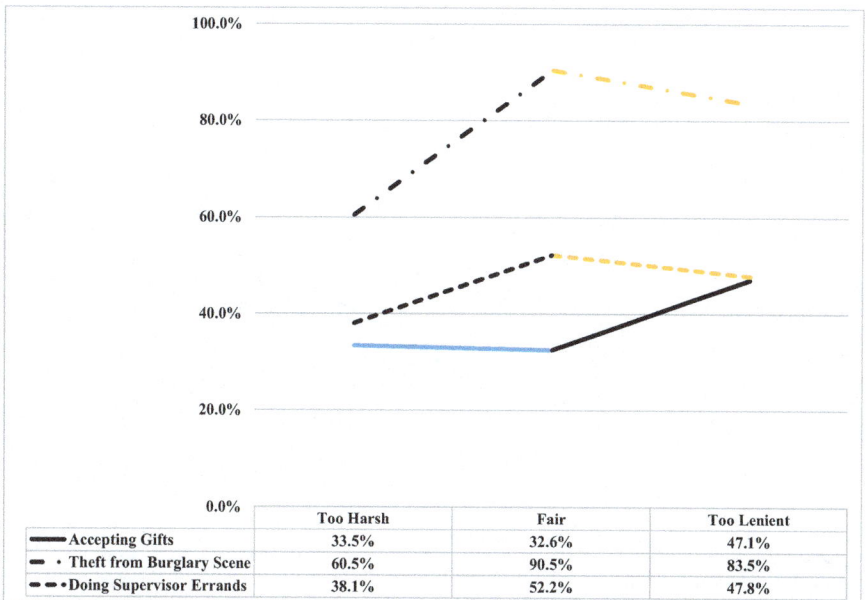

Fig. 3.2 Willingness to report based on perceptions of disciplinary fairness for corruption scenarios

fairness. These results are shown in Fig. 3.2 for corruption scenarios, Fig. 3.3 for excessive use of force scenarios, Fig. 3.4 for organizational deviance scenarios, and Fig. 3.5 for interpersonal deviance scenarios.

Starting with the *police corruption* scenarios (Fig. 3.2), two of the three scenarios follow the simple justice model (Kutnjak Ivković & Klockars, 1998). Specifically, police officers are significantly more willing to say that they would report theft from a crime scene and supervisory corruption when the expected discipline is evaluated as fair than when the expected discipline is evaluated as too harsh.

However, when the discipline is thought to be too lenient compared to fair, police officers appear less willing to report in these two scenarios, although the effect is not statistically significant. Furthermore, there are indications of discipline indifference for the scenario of accepting free gifts between too harsh and fair discipline. This is supported by the fact that police officers are most likely to report when they feel the discipline will be too lenient, suggesting that officers may not find this scenario particularly serious and thus are generally unwilling to report this misconduct if they perceive that there would be serious consequences.

Similarly, Fig. 3.3 also contains the relationship for the *use of excessive force* scenarios. In two of the three scenarios, officers' willingness to report follows the pattern predicted by the simple justice model—police officers who evaluated the expected discipline as fair were more likely to say they would report than officers who evaluated the expected discipline as too harsh. The only scenario in regard to which we do not see a significant increase in the willingness to report is the scenario

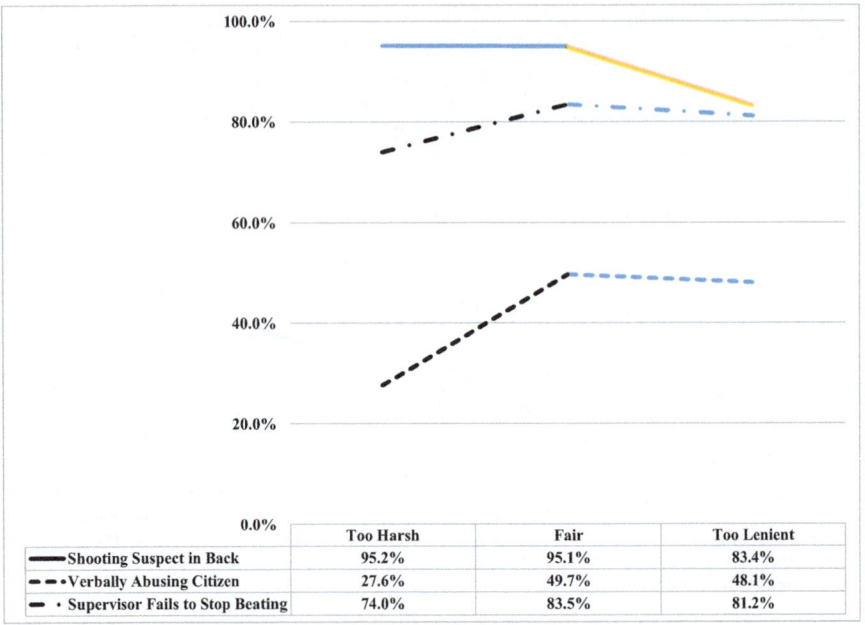

Fig. 3.3 Willingness to report based on perceptions of disciplinary fairness for excessive use of force scenarios

depicting the shooting of an unarmed suspect. In this scenario, the overwhelming majority of police officers in our sample, regardless of whether they perceived the expected discipline as too harsh or fair, said that they would report such misconduct.

There is relatively little change between the willingness to report for those who expected a fair discipline and those who felt that the discipline would be too lenient for the scenarios depicting verbal abuse of a citizen and a supervisor who failed to stop a beating. On the other hand, perceptions of lenient discipline decrease the likelihood that an officer would be willing to report the shooting of an unarmed suspect.

Figure 3.4 depicts the same willingness to report by perceptions of disciplinary fairness for *organizational deviance*. A comparison of the police officers' willingness to report for the three scenarios depicting organizational deviance (covering up DUI crash, false sick report, false overtime reporting) shows that the simple justice model fits all of these scenarios well, with the respondents who evaluated the expected discipline as fair being more likely to say that they would report than the respondents who evaluated the expected discipline as too harsh.

The other side of the graph—comparing the expressed willingness to report by the respondents who evaluated the expected discipline as fair with those who evaluated it as too lenient—yielded more diversity in their views. In two scenarios (covering up DUI crash, false sick report), the percentages were similar across these two groups, with the respondents who evaluated the expected discipline as too lenient

Results   47

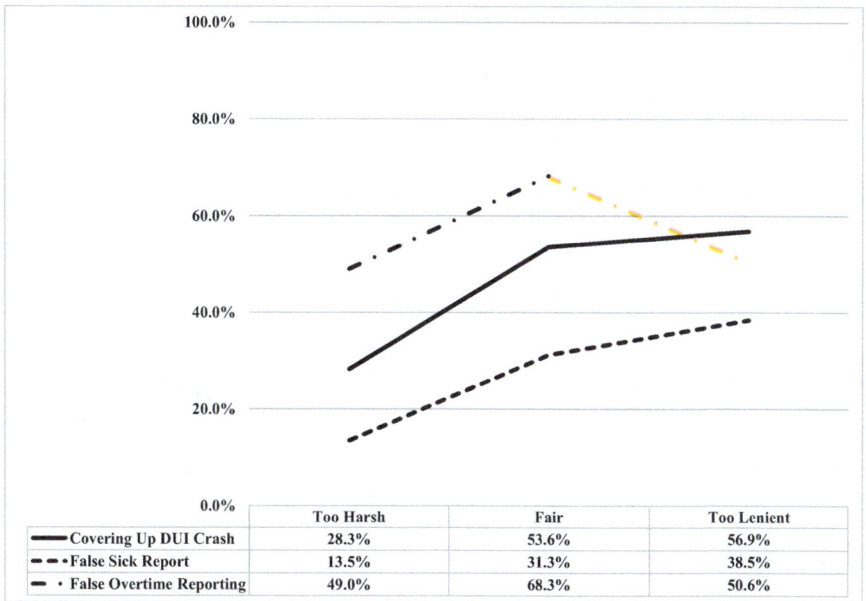

Fig. 3.4 Willingness to report based on perceptions of disciplinary fairness for organizational deviance scenarios

being somewhat more likely to say that they would report than the respondents who perceived the expected discipline as fair. Finally, the simplified deterrence model fit best the findings for the scenario describing false overtime reporting. In particular, the respondents who perceived that the expected discipline is fair were more likely to say that they would report than the respondents who perceived the expected discipline as too lenient were.

We have also compared the views of the respondents who evaluated the expected discipline as too harsh with those who evaluated the expected discipline as fair for *interpersonal deviance* scenarios (Fig. 3.5). The results show the effect for the simple justice model for all three of these scenarios, although the effect is not significant for the scenarios of yelling at coworkers and spreading false rumors about a coworker.

Focus on the comparison between the views expressed by the respondents who evaluated the expected discipline as fair the views expressed by those who evaluated the expected discipline as too lenient reveals that in two scenarios—telling sexist jokes and yelling at coworkers—the percentage of officers willing to report is greater for those who feel that the expected discipline is too lenient than for those who evaluate the expected discipline as fair.

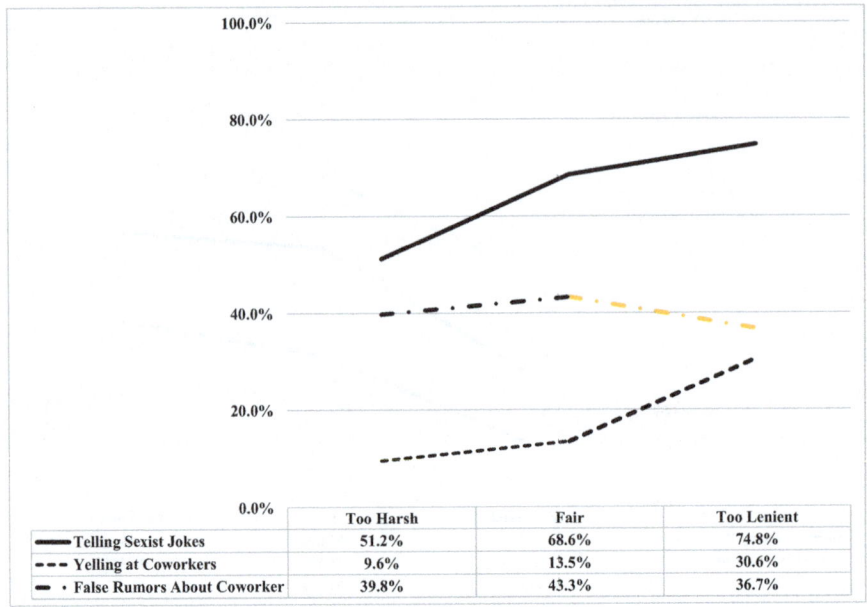

Fig. 3.5 Willingness to report based on perceptions of disciplinary fairness for interpersonal deviance scenarios

The Effects of Discipline Fairness and Police Integrity Measures on the Code of Silence

Next, we present the results from the multivariate models estimating the effect of adhering to the code of silence after considering the perceptions of disciplinary fairness. These results are building on the traditional police integrity variables. Accordingly, all estimates are net of the traditional police integrity variables presented and described in Chap. 2. We present the results for each of the scenario types below. We specifically comment on how the results compare to those presented in Chap. 2 (i.e., the unconditional police integrity estimates).

Police Corruption

We start by looking at the results from the disciplinary fairness variables on the corruption scenarios. These results are presented in Table 3.1. Expecting lenient discipline, compared to expecting fair discipline, decreases adherence to the code of silence for the scenario depicting accepting free gifts (OR = 0.35, $p < 0.001$) and the scenario depicting supervisory corruption (OR = 0.13, $p < 0.001$). Additionally, expecting harsh discipline, compared to expecting fair discipline, is associated with an increase in the adherence to the code of silence (OR = 3.82, $p < 0.001$) in the

Table 3.1 Disciplinary fairness and police integrity variables predicting code of silence

	Corruption			Excessive force			Organizational deviance			Interpersonal deviance		
	Gifts	Theft from burglary	Supervisor errands	Shooting suspect in the back	Verbally abusing citizen	Failing to report beating	Covering up DUI crash	False sick report	False overtime reporting	Telling sexist jokes	Yelling at coworkers	Spreading false rumors about coworker
Lenient discipline[a]	0.35***	1.08	0.13***	0.04***	1.06	0.56	0.67	0.10***	0.77	0.27***	0.08***	0.89
Harsh discipline[a]	0.81	3.82***	0.62	0.27	41.16***	4.14***	1.52	4.16***	1.39	2.80***	20.86***	0.47
Others' code of silence	13.64***	38.43***	14.98***	26.89***	50.15***	36.91***	39.89***	54.52***	84.15***	56.14***	44.33***	14.90***
Violation of policy	0.45***	–	0.64*	0.03***	0.26***	1.61	0.75*	0.82	2.38***	1.11	2.86***	0.33***
Own perceptions of seriousness	0.34***	–	0.85	0.01***	0.47***	0.04***	0.21***	0.11***	0.05***	0.31***	0.12***	0.73*
No discipline[b]	3.41***	12.38***	3.81***	0.01***	7.62***	0.80	0.74	83.81***	1.44	4.47***	7.99***	2.05**
Dismissal[b]	1.55	0.92	3.28***	0.33*	4.76	2.44*	0.68	0.16***	1.35	2.80	1.16	10.18*
χ^2 (df)	410.65 (7)	254.04 (5)	407.13 (7)	81.83 (7)	308.00 (7)	278.40 (7)	319.61 (7)	263.75 (7)	274.33 (7)	305.90 (7)	149.26 (7)	185.62 (7)

– parameters excluded due to collinearity
* $p < 0.05$, ** $p < 0.01$, *** $p < 0.001$
[a]Reference category is "fair discipline"
[b]Reference category is "intermediate discipline"

scenario depicting theft from a burglary scene. No other significant effects are noted for the disciplinary fairness variables in scenarios with police corruption.

Next, we look at how the results from these revised models affected the parameter estimates from the unconditional models (i.e., those with only the police integrity variables). Overall, we see that the results remain substantively unchanged for the effects of others' adherence to the code of silence, violation of policy, and perceptions of seriousness for all three scenarios. These findings suggest that the inclusion of these additional variables does not affect the variance explained by these three traditional police integrity variables. At the same time, we see that the effects of the type of expected discipline for engaging in these acts are substantively similar, although slightly augmented, from the unconditional models for the accepting free gifts and supervisory corruption scenarios. Likewise, the substantive conclusion for the type of expected discipline is consistent for theft from a burglary scene, although the effect is attenuated by 25.38% from the unconditional model. This would suggest a large portion of the variance of the type of expected discipline is associated with how fair that discipline is thought to be.

Use of Excessive Force

Next, we turn to the results for the scenarios depicting the use of excessive force. These results are also presented in Table 3.1. Expecting a lenient discipline, compared to expecting a fair discipline, reduces the likelihood that an officer will adhere to the code of silence net of other factors in the scenario of shooting an unarmed person in the back (OR = 0.04, $p < 0.001$). The same effect is not present for the other two scenarios in this category. Instead, perceptions of harsh discipline, relative to fair discipline, increase adherence to the code of silence for the scenarios involving verbal abuse of a citizen (OR = 41.16, $p < 0.001$) and failing to report a beating (OR = 4.14, $p < 0.001$).

Now we compare the results for the traditional police integrity variables from these updated models to the unconditional models presented in Chap. 2. Again, we see that, substantively, the results remain the same for others' adherence to the code of silence, although the magnitude of the effect is attenuated by 84.43% for the scenario depicting the shooting a suspect in the back, 39.71% for verbally abusing a citizen, and 72.66% for failing to report a beating. The effects for violation of policy and perceptions of seriousness remain substantively unchanged and similar in magnitude to those from the unconditional model. Additionally, the effects for the type of discipline expected remain unchanged with the addition of the new variables, although it attenuated some of the effects from the unconditional models. Also, the addition of the discipline fairness variables now yields a significant effect for dismissal (compared to intermediary discipline) in the scenario depicting shooting a suspect in the back (OR = 0.33, $p < 0.05$).

Overall, these results suggest that the inclusion of the disciplinary fairness variables into the model explains some of the variance associated with traditional police integrity variables. Furthermore, the results indicate that officers' willingness to report—or not, as is the case here—is associated with the type of discipline that will be meted out and how fair the officer evaluates that discipline to be. Finally, these results suggest that, while disciplinary fairness and type of discipline are somewhat related, they exert independent effects on an officer's willingness to report.

Organizational Deviance

We now examine the results of the models for the scenarios depicting organizational deviance, presented in Table 3.1. Here, the only scenario in which disciplinary fairness exerts an effect is the scenario depicting a false sick report. In this scenario, lenient discipline, compared to fair discipline, reduces adherence to the code of silence (OR = 0.10, $p < 0.001$); and harsh discipline, relative to fair discipline, increases adherence to the code of silence (OR = 4.16, $p < 0.001$). The direction of the effects is consistent for the other two scenarios, although the effects are not statistically significant.

Turning to the changes in the traditional police integrity variables from Chap. 2, we see that the effect of others' adherence to the code of silence is reduced by 40.9% for the scenario depicting a false sick report; however, the effect of this variable is slightly augmented for the other two scenarios. The assessment of whether an act is a violation of policy and the effect of own perceptions of seriousness are substantively unchanged in these three scenarios with the inclusion of the new variables. Finally, the effects for the type of expected discipline remain unchanged for the covering up of the DUI crash and the false overtime reporting scenarios. However, the effect of no discipline, compared to intermediary discipline, is 203% stronger (OR = 83.81, $p < 0.001$) for the false sick report after including the perception of disciplinary fairness variables. Similarly, the effect of dismissal relative to intermediary discipline is augmented by 36% (OR = 0.16, $p < 0.001$) from the unconditional model.

Interpersonal Deviance

Finally, we examine the results of the models for the scenarios depicting interpersonal deviance, also presented in Table 3.1. Here, there is a more consistent pattern of results for two of the three scenarios. Specifically, for the scenarios depicting telling sexist jokes (OR = 0.27, $p < 0.001$) and yelling at coworkers (OR = 0.08, $p < 0.001$), the effect of lenient discipline compared to fair discipline reduces adherence to the code of silence. Likewise, harsh discipline, relative to fair discipline, increases adherence to the code of silence for both the sexist joke (OR = 2.80, $p < 0.001$) and the yelling at coworkers (OR = 20.86, $p < 0.001$) scenarios. However, there is no effect for either variable in the scenario depicting spreading false rumors about coworkers.

Lastly, we compare the results of the traditional police integrity variables on the adherence to the code of silence after the inclusion of these two new variables. The results here suggest that the effects for others' perceived adherence to the code of silence, violation of policy, and the police officer's own perceptions of seriousness remain substantively unchanged. However, the effect of others' perceived adherence to the code of silence has been augmented by 84.63% with the inclusion of the disciplinary fairness variables. Similarly, many of the effects of the discipline type have been augmented with the inclusion of disciplinary fairness. Again, this would suggest that, while these two may be related, they are exerting independent effects on adherence to the code of silence for the interpersonal deviance scenarios.

Conclusion

We follow the theoretical approach outlined by Klockars and Kutnjak Ivković (Kutnjak Ivković & Klockars, 1998) to assess the relationship between the expressed willingness to report misconduct and perceptions of disciplinary fairness. This approach allowed us to examine the bivariate effect of the police officers' evaluations of expected discipline as too harsh or too lenient on their own expressed willingness to report.

Our comparison of the expressed willingness to report misconduct between the respondents who evaluated the expected discipline as fair and the respondents who evaluated the expected discipline as too harsh readily yielded the "big picture." In the majority of the scenarios (9 out of 12 in bivariate models and 6 out of 12 in multivariate models), the respondents who evaluated the expected discipline as too harsh were less likely to say that they would report the misconduct than were the respondents who evaluated the expected discipline as fair. Put differently, our results constitute substantial evidence of the simple justice model at work, both in general and across different forms of police misconduct. Our findings fit well with the results of several earlier studies (e.g., Datzer et al., 2019; Kutnjak Ivković & Klockars, 1998; Kutnjak Ivković et al., 2016b; Kutnjak Ivković & Shelley, 2007; 2010).

At the same time, we found no evidence of the simple deterrence model—assuming that harsher discipline would lead to more reporting—that would justify the use of harsh measures just to get police officers to report on the misconduct of their fellow officers. In fact, our findings provide ample evidence for police administrators that increasing the harshness of discipline—without teaching the police officers why this would be appropriate and securing their support for such measures—would be counterproductive and would backfire in the long run.

Our results also show that, in the majority of the scenarios (8 out of 12 for bivariate models and 6 out of 12 for multivariate models), whether the expected discipline is evaluated as fair or viewed as too lenient makes little difference for the police officers' expressed willingness to report misconduct, thus fitting the discipline indifference model. Such results should not be surprising because most of the extant research findings seem consistent with the model of discipline indifference (Datzer et al., 2019; Kutnjak Ivković & Klockars, 1998; Kutnjak Ivković et al., 2016b; Kutnjak Ivković & Sauerman, 2013; Kutnjak Ivković & Shelley, 2005; 2007, 2010).

The story of disciplinary fairness and its relationship with the code of silence is but one aspect of how police officers may feel about the way their organizations are treating them. In terms of the outcomes, distributive justice could include not only fair discipline, but also fair assignment allocation, promotion, and shift work. In addition to the outcomes themselves, police officers' willingness to stick to the code of silence could be linked with how they perceive that they are treated by their immediate supervisors. In the next chapter, we tackle the issue of organizational justice and its effects on the police officers' reporting decisions.

References

Alain, M. (2004). An exploratory study of Quebec's police officers' attitudes toward ethical dilemmas. In C. B. Klockars, S. Kutnjak Ivković, & M. R. Haberfeld (Eds.), *The contours of police integrity* (pp. 40–56). Sage.

Cheloukhine, S., Kutnjak Ivković, S., Haq, Q., & Haberfeld, M. R. (2015). Police integrity in Russia. In S. Kutnjak Ivković & M. Haberfeld (Eds.), *Police integrity across the world.* Springer.

Datzer, D., Kutnjak Ivković, S., Mujanović, E., & Morgan, S. (2019). A complex relation between the code of silence and education. In S. Kutnjak Ivković & M. Haberfeld (Eds.), *Exploring police integrity: Novel approaches to police integrity theory and methodology.* Springer.

Edelbacher, M., & Kutnjak Ivković, S. (2004). Ethics and the police: Studying police integrity in Austria. In C. B. Klockars, S. Kutnjak Ivković, & M. R. Haberfeld (Eds.), *The contours of police integrity* (pp. 19–39). Sage.

Haberfeld, M.R. (2004). The Heritage of Police Misconduct: The Case of the Polish Police. In Klockars, C. B., Kutnjak Ivković, S., & M. R. Haberfeld (Eds.). *The Contours of Police Integrity.* Thousand Oaks, CA: Sage Publications. pp. 95–210.

Khechumyan, A., & Kutnjak Ivković, S. (2015). Police integrity in Armenia. In S. Kutnjak Ivković & M. Haberfeld (Eds.), *Police integrity across the world.* Springer.

Klockars, C. B., & Kutnjak Ivković, S. (2004). Measuring police integrity. In M. Hickman, A. R. Piquero, & J. R. Greene (Eds.), *Police integrity and ethics.* Wadsworth.

Klockars, C. B., Kutnjak Ivković, S., Harver, W. E., & Haberfeld, M. R. (1997). *The measurement of police integrity.* Final report submitted to the U.S. Department of Justice, Office of Justice Programs, National Institute of Justice.

Klockars, C. B., Kutnjak Ivković, S., Harver, W. E., & Haberfeld, M. R. (2000). *The measurement of police integrity, NIJ research in brief.* National Institute of Justice.

Klockars, C. B., Kutnjak Ivković, S., & Haberfeld, M. R. (Eds.). (2004). *The contours of police integrity.* Sage.

Klockars, C. B., Kutnjak Ivković, S., & Haberfeld, M. R. (2006). *Enhancing police integrity.* Springer.

Kutnjak Ivković, S., & Khechumyan, A. (2014). Measuring police integrity among urban and rural police in Armenia: From local results to global implications. *International Journal of Comparative and Applied Criminal Justice, 38*(1), 39–61.

Kutnjak Ivković, S., & Klockars, C. B. (1998). The code of silence and the Croatian police. In M. Pagon (Ed.), *Policing in central and Eastern Europe: Organizational, managerial, and human resource aspects* (pp. 329–347). College of Police and Security Studies.

Kutnjak Ivković, S., & Sauerman, A. (2013). Curtailing the code of silence among the South African police. *Policing: An International Journal of Police Strategies and Management, 36*(1), 175–198.

Kutnjak Ivković, S., & Shelley, T. O. (2005). The Bosnian police and police integrity: A continuing story. *European Journal of Criminology, 2*(4), 428–454.

Kutnjak Ivković, S., & Shelley, T. O. (2007). Police Integrity and the Czech Police Officers. *International Journal of Comparative and Applied Criminal Justice, 31*(1), 21–49.

Kutnjak Ivković, S., & Shelley, T. O. (2008). The police code of silence and different paths toward democratic policing. *Policing and Society, 18*(4), 445–473.

Kutnjak Ivković, S., & Shelley, T. O. (2010). The code of silence and disciplinary fairness: A comparison of Czech police supervisor and line officer views. *Policing: An International Journal of Police Strategies and Management, 33*(3), 548–574.

Kutnjak Ivković, S., Cajner Mraović, I., & Borovec, K. (2016a). An empirical test of the influence of society at large on police integrity in a centralized police system. *Policing: An International Journal of Police Strategies and Management, 39*(2), 302–318.

Kutnjak Ivković, S., Peacock, R., & Haberfeld, M. (2016b). Does discipline fairness matter for the police code of silence? Answers from the U.S. supervisors and line officers. *Policing: An International Journal of Police Strategies and Management, 39*(2), 354–369.

Kutnjak Ivković, S., Haberfeld, M. R., Cajner Mraović, I., Prpić, M., Hamm, J. A., & Wolfe, S. (2019). Seriousness of police (mis)behavior and organizational justice. In S. Kutnjak Ivković & M. Haberfeld (Eds.), *Exploring police integrity: Novel approaches to police integrity theory and methodology*. Springer.

Lobnikar, B., & Meško, G. (2015). Police integrity in Slovenia. In S. Kutnjak Ivković & M. Haberfeld (Eds.), *Police integrity across the world*. Springer.

Peacock, R., Prpić, M., Kutnjak Ivković, S., Cajner Mraović, I., & Božović, V. (2020). Shades of blue: Exploring the code of silence in Croatia and Serbia. *International Journal of Comparative and Applied Criminal Justice*. https://doi.org/10.1080/01924036.2020.1824872

Porter, L. E., Prenzler, T., & Hine, K. (2015). Police integrity in Australia. In S. Kutnjak Ivković & M. Haberfeld (Eds.), *Measuring police integrity across the world*. Springer.

Pounti, A., Vuorinen, S., & Kutnjak Ivković, S. (2004). Sustaining police integrity in Finland. In C. B. Klockars, S. Kutnjak Ivković, & M. R. Haberfeld (Eds.), *The contours of police integrity* (pp. 95–115). Sage.

Punch, M., Huberts, L. W. J. C., & Lamboo, M. E. D. (2004). Integrity, perceptions, and investigations in the Netherlands. In C. B. Klockars, S. Kutnjak Ivković, & M. R. Haberfeld (Eds.), *The contours of police integrity* (pp. 161–175). Sage.

Sauerman, A., & Kutnjak Ivković, S. (2015). Police integrity in South Africa. In S. Kutnjak Ivković & M. Haberfeld (Eds.), *Police integrity across the world*. Springer.

Torstensson Levander, M., & Ekenvall, B. (2004). Homogeneity in moral standards in Swedish police culture. In C. B. Klockars, S. Kutnjak Ivković, & M. R. Haberfeld (Eds.), *The contours of police integrity* (pp. 251–265). Sage.

Vallmüür, B. (2015). Police integrity in Estonia. In S. Kutnjak Ivković & M. Haberfeld (Eds.), *Police integrity across the world*. Springer.

Vallmüür, B. (2019). The contours of an organizational theory of green police integrity. In S. Kutnjak Ivković & M. Haberfeld (Eds.), *Exploring police integrity*. Springer.

Van Droogenbroeck, F., Spruyt, B., Kutnjak Ivković, S., & Haberfeld, M. R. (2019). The effects of ethics training on police integrity. In S. Kutnjak Ivković & M. Haberfeld (Eds.), *Exploring police integrity: Novel approaches to police integrity theory and methodology*. Springer.

Westmarland, L. (2004). Policing integrity: Britain's thin blue line. In C. B. Klockars, S. Kutnjak Ivković, & M. R. Haberfeld (Eds.), *The contours of police integrity* (pp. 75–93). Sage.

References

Westmarland, L. (2006). Police ethics and integrity: Breaking the blue code of silence. *Policing and Society, 15*(2), 145–165.

Wu, G., & Makin, D. A. (2019). The quagmire that is an unwillingness to report: Situating the code of silence within the Chinese police context. *Criminal Justice and Behavior, 46*(4), 608–627.

Open Access This chapter is licensed under the terms of the Creative Commons Attribution 4.0 International License (http://creativecommons.org/licenses/by/4.0/), which permits use, sharing, adaptation, distribution and reproduction in any medium or format, as long as you give appropriate credit to the original author(s) and the source, provide a link to the Creative Commons license and indicate if changes were made.

The images or other third party material in this chapter are included in the chapter's Creative Commons license, unless indicated otherwise in a credit line to the material. If material is not included in the chapter's Creative Commons license and your intended use is not permitted by statutory regulation or exceeds the permitted use, you will need to obtain permission directly from the copyright holder.

Chapter 4
The Code of Silence and Organizational Justice

Abstract This chapter focuses on how the police officers' willingness to report is shaped by their perceptions of organizational justice. With a few exceptions, bivariate analyses revealed a negative relationship between the adherence to the code of silence and the perceptions of organizational justice. Multivariate analyses indicated that the effect of perceived organizational justice varies across the types of scenarios. While the effect of organizational justice on the adherence to the code of silence is negative for the corruption scenarios, organizational justice exerts an inconsistent relationship on the adherence to the code of silence for organizational deviance scenarios and interpersonal deviance scenarios. Yet, the perceptions of organizational justice seem to have no effect on the use of excessive force scenarios. Additionally, the estimated other police officers' adherence to the code of silence is the strongest predictor of an officer's own adherence to the code of silence.

Keywords Police conduct · Code of silence · Police integrity · Organizational justice · Organizational commitment · Procedural justice · Distributive justice · Interactional justice

Introduction

Like any other organizations, police agencies have significant effects on work behaviors, perceptions, attitudes, emotions, and orientations of their employees. Police officers are subject to decisions made by their supervisors, and these decisions involve professional, economic, and social implications for the officers. In return, attitudes of the employees toward their organizations also affect certain work-related outcomes. Officers' perceptions of their organizations could shape their job satisfaction, rule adherence, officer-citizen encounters, engagement in misconduct, quality and quantity of work, likelihood of staying with the organization, and commitment to the organization. The notion of organizational justice has been shown to be a key factor regarding the relationship between the employees and their organizations. A large body of empirical evidence within organizational justice, criminology/criminal justice, and organizational behavior/management scholarship indicates that perceived organizational justice is a positive predictor of beneficial workplace attitudes and behaviors (Donner et al., 2015; Kutnjak Ivković & Sauerman, 2016; Kutnjak Ivković & Klockars, 1998; Kutnjak Ivković & Shelley, 2010; Tyler et al., 2007; Wolfe & Lawson, 2020).

A review of the literature reveals that police officers who believe that they receive fair treatment by their supervisors have higher levels of productivity, job satisfaction, and commitment to their organizations (Cohen-Charash & Spector, 2001; Farmer et al., 2003, Frear et al., 2018). Conversely, officers who perceived that they have experienced organizational injustice are more likely to engage in misconduct and adhere to the code of silence (Myhill & Bradford, 2013; Tankebe & Meško, 2014; Wolfe & Lawson, 2020; Wolfe & Piquero, 2011). Studies of perceived organizational justice among police personnel in several countries yielded similar results (Carless, 2006; Crow et al., 2012; Haberfeld & Kutnjak Ivković, 2015; Wu & Maken, 2019).

This chapter explores the nature of the relationship between organizational justice and the code of silence. In particular, we examine how organizational justice shapes the police officers' perceptions and their willingness to report misconduct. A two-step analysis is utilized to test these organizational effects on the code of silence. In the first step of our study, we utilize bivariate analyses to test whether organizational justice is related to the code of silence. In the second step, we employ multivariate analyses to test the effects of the organizational justice on the police officers' adherence to the code of silence while controlling for traditional police integrity measures.

Organizational Justice

Colquitt (2001) suggested that organizational justice consists of four distinct dimensions. These dimensions are distributive justice, procedural justice, interpersonal justice, and informational justice. *Distributive justice* refers to the fairness of decision outcomes (Adams, 1965; Colquitt, 2001; Deutsch, 1975; Homans, 1961; Leventhal, 1976). It is about the justice in the distribution of organizational resources. *Procedural justice* refers to "justice of the processes that lead to decision outcomes" (Colquitt, 2001: 386). Procedural justice is attained by giving employees a voice in the decision-making process or influence over the decision outcomes, or by commitment to just process elements (Thibaut & Walker, 1975). A fair decision-making process should involve consistency, lack of bias, correctability, representation, accuracy, and ethicality (Leventhal, 1980; Leventhal et al., 1980). *Interpersonal justice* refers to the level of respect and propriety that employees receive from their supervisors (Colquitt, 2001). *Informational justice* refers to the way employees are treated by their supervisors. It is about whether supervisors treat their subordinates with dignity, respect, in a polite manner, and without improper remarks or comments (Colquitt, 2001).

Effects of Organizational Justice on Police Attitudes and Behavior

The relationship between organizational justice and organizational outcomes in corporate environments has been examined by several studies (Bechtoldt et al., 2007; Byrne, 2005; Cohen-Charash & Spector, 2001; Colquitt et al., 2001). The research has demonstrated that corporate employees who experience fair behaviors from their supervisors are more likely to engage in positive organizational behaviors, and show greater job satisfaction and productivity (Ambrose & Schminke, 2009; Byrne, 2005; McFarlin & Sweeney, 1992). The research has also indicated that the existence of organizational justice in corporate environments tends to reduce the number of behaviors that are in conflict with organizational rules, goals, and expectations (Colquitt et al., 2002; Fox et al., 2001).

Organizational justice means more to police officers and correctional officers compared to corporate employees (Wolfe & Lawson, 2020). Because police officers and correctional officers are exposed to danger on a daily basis, are accountable for their wrongdoings, and are expected to respond to a variety of problems, they have to deal with a significant amount of uncertainty (Wolfe et al., 2018). Wolfe et al. (2018) argue that organizational justice greatly helps police officers and correctional officers to handle this uncertainty. Thus, organizational justice has been considered to be an important predictor of positive and negative work attitudes and behaviors among criminal justice employees.

Cohen-Charash and Spector (2001) suggest that organizational justice has effects on the attitudes of the employees and, therefore, influences job performance. Lind and Tyler (1988) found a positive correlation between perceived organizational justice and employee's evaluation of the organization, commitment, and loyalty to the organization. In another illustrative study, Rosenbaum and McCarty (2017) revealed that, when the officers observe higher levels of organization-wide, supervisory, leadership, and diversity justice, they display higher levels of positive behaviors (i.e., organizational commitment, job satisfaction, and rule compliance).

Indeed, organizational justice is perceived to be positively associated with desirable behavior in police agencies (Kutnjak Ivković & Saueman, 2016; Kutnjak Ivković & Shelley, 2010; Wolfe & Piquero, 2011). Tyler et al. (2007) found that police officers who report positive views of organizational justice were more likely to follow organizational rules and defer to organizational policies. Similarly, Haas et al. (2015) found a positive correlation between fair treatment by the supervisors and police officers' compliance with agency policies. Rothwell and Baldwin (2007) also found a positive relationship between perceived organizational justice and willingness to report police misconduct. Similarly, Kutnjak Ivković and Sauerman (2016) found that South African police officers who felt there was procedural justice in police disciplinary processes were less likely to say that they would adhere to the code of silence.

The research findings have consistently demonstrated a positive association between perceptions of organizational justice and adherence to rules and policies of the agencies (Bradford et al., 2014; Haas et al., 2015; Kutnjak Ivković & Shelley, 2010; Kutnjak Ivković & Sauerman, 2016; Reynolds & Helfers, 2019; Rothwell & Baldwin, 2007; Tyler et al., 2007, Wolfe & Piquero, 2011). Several studies have attempted to explain why this association exists, and have found that attitudes of the officers toward their organizations might have a potential mediating effect on the association between organizational justice and rule adherence (Cohen-Charash & Spector, 2001; Colquitt et al., 2001; Dick, 2011; Lind & Tyler, 1988; Tankebe, 2010). Some researchers have argued that organizational commitment serves as a potential mediating mechanism (Fridell et al., 2020; Lind & Tyler, 1988).

Farmer et al. (2003) studied the perceptions of American police officers and found a positive correlation between organizational justice and organizational commitment. Subsequent studies found additional evidence that perceived organizational justice is positively related to organizational commitment among police officers in Australia (Carless, 2006) and South Korea (Crow et al., 2012). In their meta-review, Donner et al. (2015) documented that perceptions of organizational justice are positively correlated not only with organizational commitment, but also with job satisfaction, trust in the administration, compliance with decisions, and willingness to report misconduct. Similarly, perceived fairness of organizational decision-making process has been found to have a significant effect on trust in the agency, job satisfaction, organizational commitment, and desire to stay with the agency (Crow et al., 2012; De Angelis & Kupchik, 2007; Myhill & Bradford, 2013; Wolfe & Piquero, 2011).

Additionally, research on organizational justice has found significant evidence indicating a correlation between procedural justice during the selection process and fairness of the screening test. For example, Truxillo et al. (2002) explored the perceptions of police applicants in the Southern USA about their experiences during the recruitment and selection stage. Truxillo and colleagues' findings (2002) revealed a positive association between perceived procedural justice in the selection process and fairness of the screening test/timeliness of the feedback. Carless (2006) examined the perceptions of police applicants in Australia and found a positive relationship between perceived procedural justice during the selection process and perceived outcome fairness. Farmer et al. (2003) found a positive correlation between perceived fairness and decision-making in the selection process of undercover officers. Crow et al. (2012) also found a positive relationship between perceived organizational justice and decision-making in job rewards and performance evaluations.

Furthermore, extant research suggests that police officers who believe their supervisors are fair in their organizational behaviors are more likely to treat citizens with procedural justice (Tankebe, 2014). Van Craen and Skogan (2017) also explored the effects of internal procedural justice on officer-citizen interactions, and found that when police officers receive fair treatment from their supervisors, they are more likely to follow the procedural justice concepts of "respect," "voice," and "accountability" in their interactions with citizens. Along the same lines, research by Bradford et al. (2014) yielded evidence that British police officers' perceptions of organizational justice are associated with an increase in their positive views of community policing and with greater self-reported compliance.

Organizational Justice and the Code of Silence

While prior studies have tested the effect of organizational justice on police attitudes and behavior in general, no prior study of which we are aware has directly tested its effects on the police officers' code of silence. Yet, numerous researchers and theorists have reported a negative correlation between organizational justice and deviant behaviors/police misconduct (Bradford et al., 2014; Haas et al., 2015; Kutnjak Ivković & Sauerman, 2016; Tyler et al., 2007: Wolfe & Piquero, 2011), thus suggesting that the protection of police misconduct committed by fellow officers should also be related to organizational justice.

Previous research has shown that employees who feel they are not fairly treated are more likely to engage in retaliatory behavior (Barclay et al., 2005), theft (Colquitt, et al., 2006), cyberloafing (Lim, 2002), and harmful behavior to organizational property (Colquitt et al., 2001). As a negative workplace behavior, police misconduct has been an issue of great concern in contemporary societies (Fridell et al., 2020; Lersch, 2002; Palmiotto, 2001; Van Craen & Skogan, 2017). Because of its potential to produce adverse consequences for the individual officer, the individual citizen, the community, and the police profession, the issue of police misconduct was one of the driving forces behind the creation of the President's Task Force on 21st Century Policing in the United States (2015). The final report (2015) of the President's Task Force suggests that procedural justice within the police organizations is an important facet of addressing the issue of police misconduct.

Van Craen and Skogan (2017) also noted that officers' direct supervisors are of crucial importance in police organizations because their behaviors shape the officers' perceptions, including their perceptions of organizational justice. If they are not fair and rule-bound, officers are more likely to display negative behaviors in their interactions with citizens. In line with this, research by Haas et al. (2015) explored non-compliance by police officers. They studied the perceptions of police officers of the Metropolitan Police in Buenos Aires and found that fair treatment by supervisors and fair decision-making may facilitate the implementation of organizational policies and contribute to a reduction in police misconduct.

Wolfe and Piquero (2011) explored the effects of organizational justice on police officers in Philadelphia; they found a negative correlation between organizational justice and noble-cause corruption, citizen complaints, number of internal affairs investigations, and number of departmental charges. Furthermore, results from Tankebe's (2014) study showed a negative association between organizational justice and the use of force. Not surprisingly, the findings of Donner et al. (2015) also revealed a negative relationship between organizational justice and police officers' determination to engage in police misconduct. In their study of the relationship between organizational justice and police officer attitudes toward misconduct,

Fridell et al. (2020) found a direct correlation between perceptions of organizational justice and the police officers' support for misconduct.

This Chapter

Extant research on the code of silence has demonstrated that organizational variables are the critical predictors of the police officers' expressed willingness to report, while individual characteristics do not serve as such strong predictors. In this chapter, we expand the traditional police integrity approach by incorporating the effect of organizational justice on the police officers' adherence to the code of silence. While prior studies have tested the effect of organizational justice on police attitudes and behavior in general, no prior study of which we are aware has tested its effects on the attitudes toward different forms of police misconduct, including police corruption, use of excessive force, organizational deviance, and interpersonal deviance.

Methodology

Sample

In the later 2010s, we have surveyed police officers from a medium-size municipal police agency in the United States. Our sample includes 148 sworn police officers. For characteristics of our sample and police agency, please see Chaps. 1 and 2.

Measures

The analyses presented in this chapter explore the effects of organizational justice on the respondents' expressed willingness to report misconduct. Our measures of police integrity, including the code of silence, come from the new version of the police integrity questionnaire (Kutnjak Ivković et al., 2019) that includes scenarios dealing with police corruption, use of excessive force, organizational deviance, and interpersonal deviance. After the respondents read each of these 12 scenarios, they were asked to answer seven identical questions, including questions asking the respondents to assess misconduct seriousness, their familiarity with official rules, their estimates of the appropriate and expected discipline, and their willingness to report misconduct. For details, please see Chaps. 1 and 2.

Dependent Variable

The dependent variable in this chapter is the respondents' expressed *own adherence to the code of silence* for reporting misconduct. It is built upon the answers to the question asking the respondents their willingness to report misconduct described in each scenario. While answering this question, the respondents could have selected an answer from a 5-point Likert-type scale, ranging from 1 = "definitely would not report" to 5 = "definitely would report." The measure of code of silence was created by recoding the variable such that values of 1 and 2 (i.e., generally unwilling to report) were coded as a 1 with other values were coded as a 0.

Organizational Independent Variables

The organizational variables in our models include measures of the respondents' *own evaluations of misconduct seriousness*, their estimates of whether the misconduct described in the scenario *violates official rules*, their estimates of *expected discipline*, and their estimates of *most police officers' willingness to report*. For a more detailed description, please see Chap. 2.

Organizational Justice Independent Variables

The questionnaire also contained separate questions measuring various subdimensions of organizational justice, based on the study by Wolfe et al. (2018). The measure was comprised of 14 items that depicted *procedural justice* (six items), *distributive justice* (four items), and *interactional justice* (four items). The specific items and their descriptive statistics are presented in Table 4.1. For each item, the respondents could have selected one answer from a 5-point Likert scale ranging from 1 = "strongly disagree" to 5 = "strongly agree."

All items were subjected to principal axis factoring to determine how the items loaded onto latent constructs. This process initially yielded two factors that had a fair degree of conceptual overlap between both factors (i.e., a high number of double loading items). The number of double loading items suggested the factor analysis may be over-extracting factors based on the number of items (Thompson & Daniel, 1996). In essence, the algorithm is primed to identify more factors rather than fewer factors. This frequently occurs when there is a high degree of correlation between the constructs, as was the case here ($\rho = 0.57$). This is a common problem in organizational justice research (Colquitt & Shaw, 2005). To address this issue, we created a *global measure of organizational justice* comprised of all the items, which had evidence of validity (the values of λ, as shown in the last column of Table 4.1, are high, with average value of 0.71) and reliability ($\alpha = 0.93$).

Table 4.1 Organizational justice

	M (SD)	λ
Command staff apply policies in a way that promotes consistency in decisions that impact the workplace	3.31 (1.40)	0.56
Policy decisions made by command staff provide the opportunity for employees to have a voice in decisions	4.12 (1.01)	0.53
Command staff clearly explains the reasons for their decisions (i.e., policy changes)	3.72 (1.06)	0.46
My immediate supervisors consider employee viewpoints	4.23 (1.23)	0.86
My immediate supervisors conduct fair investigations of citizen complaints	4.48 (1.09)	0.87
My immediate supervisors support any lawful action or decision I make in the field	4.42 (1.13)	0.88
My immediate supervisors treat employees the same regardless of their gender	4.49 (1.14)	0.80
My immediate supervisors treat employees the same regardless of their race or ethnicity	4.58 (1.08)	0.79
Discipline is issued fairly in my agency	2.70 (1.32)	0.50
The expectation for job performance and experience to obtain promotion is reasonable in my agency	3.04 (1.26)	0.50
My immediate supervisors treat me with respect	4.44 (1.11)	0.89
I am confident I can approach my immediate supervisors with a professional issue	4.55 (1.09)	0.84
I am confident I can approach my immediate supervisors with a personal issue	4.26 (1.26)	0.80
Command staff treats employees with respect and consideration	3.72 (1.15)	0.66

($\alpha = 0.93$)

The bivariate relationship between our latent measure of organizational justice created here and the measure of disciplinary fairness (i.e., −1 for lenient punishment, 0 for fair discipline, and +1 for harsh discipline), the relationships are inconsistent across scenarios and rather modest in magnitude (i.e., $-0.15 < \rho < 0.15$). This suggests that, while the measure of disciplinary fairness may be related to the measure of organizational justice, the two measures are certainly not redundant.

Individual Independent Variables

Several variables measured the respondents' demographic characteristics: *length of service, gender, assignment, supervisory status*, and *education*. Because of the small sample size, we used these demographic characteristics as the control variables in our multivariate models. Please see Chap. 2 for details.

Analytic Strategy

The analyses again proceed in two stages. The first stage examines the relationship between our latent measure of organizational justice and adherence to the code of silence for each of the 12 scenarios. These are estimated as a series of point-biserial correlations between adherence to the code of silence (1 = yes) and the continuous measure of organizational justice. The second stage of the analyses looks at the multivariate relationships between the traditional police integrity measures, the latent measure of organizational justice created, and measures of the code of silence for each of the scenarios. The multivariate models are again estimated using the cross-folding LASSO technique for inference with the same controls as prior chapters. For additional details on this technique, please see Chap. 2.

Results

The Effects of Organizational Justice on the Code of Silence

We first analyzed the bivariate relationship between the latent measure of organizational justice created (items listed in Table 4.1) and the adherence to the code of silence for each of the scenarios (Table 4.2). The results indicate that, generally speaking, there is a negative relationship between the adherence to the code of silence and organizational justice. This is consistent with prior research on the topic of organizational misconduct (e.g., Colquitt & Shaw, 2005).

There are a few exceptions to this rule (Table 4.2). In particular, there are four scenarios (shooting suspect in back; supervisor fails to stop beating, cover-up of DUI crash, and false rumors about coworker) for which the perceptions of organizational justice and the code of silence are positively correlated, thus contraindicating the results from the prior research. However, in only two of these scenarios (shooting a suspect in the back and covering up a DUI crash) the results are statistically significant. It is unclear what is different about these scenarios compared to the others, although two of the contraindicated findings are scenarios depicting the excessive use of force.

Next, we look at the average value of ρ between organizational justice and adherence to the code of silence across the four different types of scenarios (i.e., corruption, excessive force, organizational deviance, and interpersonal deviance). The strongest and most consistent predictors are for police corruption (with the average relationship $M = -0.21$, SD = 0.04), followed by organizational deviance ($M = -0.13$, SD = 0.24), interpersonal deviance ($M = -0.07$, SD = 0.16), and, lastly, the use of excessive force ($M = -0.01$, SD = 0.26). Overall, these results suggest that organizational justice has a more consistent relationship with adherence to the code of silence for certain types of scenarios than others.

Table 4.2 Bivariate association between organizational justice variables and code of silence

	Organizational justice	
	By scenario	Average ρ value by scenario type
Corruption		−0.21
Accepting gifts	−0.22*	
Theft from burglary scene	−0.24*	
Doing supervisor errands	−0.17*	
Excessive use of force		−0.01
Shooting suspect in back	0.15*	
Verbally abusing citizen	−0.31*	
Supervisor fails to stop beating	0.12	
Organizational deviance		−0.13
Covering up DUI crash	0.14*	
False sick report	−0.24*	
False overtime reporting	−0.29*	
Interpersonal deviance		−0.07
Telling sexist jokes	−0.14*	
Yelling at coworkers	−0.18*	
False rumors about coworker	0.12	

The Effects of Organizational Justice and Police Integrity on the Code of Silence

Prior to looking at the results of the organizational justice measure, let us examine the results from the traditional police integrity measures from Chap. 2. The results are presented in Table 4.3. Overall, the results from the other police integrity measures remain relatively consistent with the findings from Chap. 2, although the addition of organizational justice does stabilize some of the estimates a bit (i.e., homogenizes the standard errors), which results in some effects being statistically significant here, but not in Chap. 2.

Police Corruption

The results for the traditional police integrity measures remain relatively consistent with the models in prior chapters. Specifically, for corruption, we note that, compared to the baseline models, we see that the substantive interpretation remains relatively consistent with the results from Chap. 2. In fact, all the same variables are significant and, apart from the effect of others' adherence to the code of silence, all other variable effects were slightly diminished compared to the baseline models. The only exception to this general rule is the strength of the relationship between the anticipated other police officers' adherence to the code of silence and officers' own adherence to the code of silence for the scenario depicting supervisory errands,

Table 4.3 Organizational justice effects on the code of silence

	Corruption			Excessive force		
	Gifts	Theft from burglary	Supervisor errands	Shooting suspect in the back	Verbally abusing citizen	Failing to report beating
Organizational justice	0.45***	0.72***	0.94	0.99	1.07	1.09
Others' code of silence	10.09***	41.60***	130.60***	53.47***	63.00***	131.43***
Violation of policy	0.33***	–	0.61***	0.07***	0.38***	1.22
Own perceptions of seriousness	0.32***	--	0.75	0.01***	0.31***	0.06***
No discipline[a]	2.05***	11.21***	2.11***	0.01***	1.62	0.62
Dismissal[a]	1.95	0.90	4.95***	0.63	7.91***	3.20**
χ^2 (df)	396.60 (6)	208.43 (4)	447.55 (6)	106.07 (6)	321.79 (6)	296.32 (6)

	Organizational deviance			Interpersonal deviance		
	Covering up DUI crash	False sick report	False overtime reporting	Telling sexist jokes	Yelling at coworkers	Spreading false rumors about coworker
Organizational justice	1.18*	0.94	0.61***	0.90	0.86	1.50***
Others' code of silence	40.73***	–	74.71***	61.72***	47.77***	29.37***
Violation of policy	0.89	0.76	2.35***	1.08	2.61***	0.37***
Own perceptions of seriousness	0.19***	0.07***	0.04***	0.27***	0.10***	0.62***
No discipline[a]	0.75	41.84***	1.04	1.92*	2.44***	2.43***
Dismissal[a]	1.03	0.17***	1.25	3.37	12.42***	9.03***
χ^2 (df)	363.24 (6)	207.44 (5)	246.63 (6)	226.48 (6)	369.89 (6)	166.80 (6)

Notes: * = $p < 0.05$, ** = $p < 0.01$, *** = $p < 0.001$; – = parameters excluded due to collinearity
[a]Reference category is "intermediate discipline"

where the effect was augmented by 50.86% with the addition of organizational justice compared to the baseline models. In other words, in the case of supervisory corruption, an officer's willingness to adhere to the code of silence—as of that of his/her peers—is strongly influenced by perceptions of organizational justice.

The effect of organizational justice on adherence to the code of silence is negative for the *corruption* scenarios, although it is statistically significant in only two of the three scenarios (gifts, theft from burglary). The effects of organizational justice are stronger in the least serious scenario (i.e., accepting free gifts; OR = 0.45, $p < 0.001$), compared to the most serious corruption scenario (i.e., theft from a crime scene; OR = 0.72, $p < 0.001$). We offer a potential explanation for this finding.

Theft from a burglary scene is typically identified as the most serious scenario by officers, and is the scenario in which the lowest percent of the officers indicated that they would not report. As such, the effect of organizational justice may be limited because of the more ubiquitous willingness to report this sort of behavior (i.e., only 5% of officers reported being *unwilling* to report this behavior). Conversely, the scenario receiving free gifts is seen as least serious and most likely to be protected by the code of silence (i.e., more than 65% of officers reported being *unwilling* to report this behavior).

Use of Excessive Force

We now turn to the effects of organizational justice on adhering to the code of silence for scenarios depicting the *use of excessive force*, also shown in Table 4.3. We start by comparing the results of the traditional measures of police integrity to those from the baseline models presented in Chap. 2. Again, we see almost the same pattern of results as those from Chap. 2, although the inclusion of the organizational justice variable slightly changes the magnitude of the effects for the traditional police integrity variables in the scenario in which a supervisor failed to report a beating. The others' perceived adherence to the code of silence remains significantly and positively associated with the respondents' own anticipated adherence to the code of silence in the new models. Furthermore, the estimated other police officers' adherence to the code of silence is the strongest predictor of an officer's own adherence to the code of silence in the use of excessive force scenarios.

Perceptions of organizational justice are unrelated, both substantively and significantly, to the adherence to the code of silence for the scenarios depicting the use of excessive force. It may be that, in these sorts of situations, the effects of organizational justice are masked by feelings about the likely fairness of the discipline that an officer is likely to receive given the national discourse about police use of force. In other words, because of the sensitive nature of police use of force in modern American society, without considering the fairness of the discipline (see Chap. 3), the effects of organizational justice may remain hidden because of the politically sensitive nature of these scenarios.

Organizational Deviance

The effects of organizational justice on adherence to the code of silence in organizational and interpersonal deviance scenarios are presented in Table 4.3. We start by examining the effects of the traditional police integrity variables and note that, after the inclusion of organizational justice, the results are similar to those from Chap. 2, with some key differences. For example, while the perceived others' adherence to the code of silence is still significantly associated with an officer's own adherence to the code of silence in these situations, the effects are diminished. Furthermore, in the scenario of a false sick report from an officer, we can no longer estimate the independent effect of others' adherence to the code of silence because it becomes a perfect or redundant predictor (i.e., those, and only those, who feel that others would not report, will not report themselves).

For the false sick report, the respondents express a greater willingness to see offenders disciplined. After all, minor discipline compared to intermediary discipline increases the risk of adherence to the code of silence, while termination compared to intermediary discipline significantly reduces adherence to the code of silence. It is unclear why for only this scenario officers express this type of sentiment. One salient and potentially relevant fact is this is the only situation in which a non-involved officer may have his/her life affected. In other words, an officer calling out sick may mean that someone else would get held over to cover for that shift or the offending officer's colleagues may be forced to work harder in his/her absence.

Next, we turn to the results of organizational justice on the adherence to the code of silence in these organizational deviance scenarios. Here, organizational justice exerts an inconsistent relationship on the adherence to the code of silence for these three scenarios. In the scenario depicting the cover-up of a DUI crash involving a fellow officer, perceptions of organizational justice are significantly related to the adherence to the code of silence (OR = 1.18, $p < 0.05$), whereas organizational justice exerts a negative effect for false reporting of overtime (OR = 0.61, $p < 0.001$) and no significant effect on reporting an officer for a false sick report.

Interpersonal Deviance

Finally, we turn to the results for interpersonal deviance, also presented in Table 4.3, and present the results for the traditional police integrity measures. There are two patterns of results of particular relevance. First, the effect of recognizing that a particular scenario is a violation of department policy exerts an inconsistent effect across scenarios. For the scenario involving yelling at coworkers, this effect is positive (OR = 2.61, $p < 0.001$). For spreading false rumors about a coworker, the effect is negative (OR = 0.37, $p < 0.001$). Finally, the effect is insignificant for the scenario depicting telling sexist jokes.

This conjecture may be supported by the second interesting finding here. Notably, officers report that any form of discipline—especially dismissal—increases adherence to the code of silence in a particular situation. In other words, these two findings may suggest that police officers may not see these scenarios as deviant and, accordingly, their decision to report is based on the perceived harm relative to the perceived likelihood in how the situation will be handled.

The effect of organizational justice is again not as consistent in these scenarios as in others. Perceptions of organizational justice should reduce the likelihood of adhering to the code of silence for telling sexist jokes and yelling at coworkers, yet they are not statistically significant. In fact, perceptions of organizational justice are only significantly associated with an increased likelihood of adhering to the code of silence in the scenario depicting spreading false rumors about a coworker

(OR = 1.50, $p < 0.001$). This finding is unexpected. Generally, in an agency in which an officer perceives higher levels of organizational justice, the officer should feel more comfortable reporting when a member of the organization is being treated unjustly by another member, but that does not seem to be the case here. Without additional data, we cannot explore what is different about this scenario relative to the others so that it causes this finding.

Conclusion

The police are given the power and authority to control the behavior of others, and they are expected to carry out their complex and difficult tasks with integrity. Although the most troublesome or tragic examples of police misconduct (e.g., the George Floyd case) constitute a small fraction of daily police-citizen interactions, police misconduct creates an aura of suspicion, mistrust, and uncertainty. Police misconduct is a serious matter whenever it occurs, and it has far-reaching consequences for the employee, the police profession, and ultimately for the whole society (Kappeler et al., 1998; Lersch, 2002). Therefore, it is essential to study the efficacy of the mechanisms that are utilized to prevent police misconduct. In this chapter, we tested the organizational justice effects on the police officers' willingness to report misconduct on the scenarios describing police corruption, use of excessive force, organizational deviance, and interpersonal deviance.

Our bivariate analyses revealed a negative relationship between organizational justice and the respondents' adherence to the code of silence in two-thirds of the scenarios (8 out of 12). This finding is consistent with the extant research (e.g., Carless, 2006; Colquitt & Shaw, 2005; Crow et al., 2012; Haberfeld & Kutnjak Ivković, 2015; Myhill & Bradford, 2013; Tankebe & Meško, 2014; Wolfe & Lawson, 2020; Wolfe & Piquero, 2011; Wu & Maken, 2019). In two of the twelve scenarios (i.e., shooting suspect in back; cover-up of DUI crash), we found a positive and statistically significant relationship between organizational justice and the adherence to the code of silence, which does not fit well with the findings reported in previous research. It is unclear why the relationship is positive in these scenarios.

Furthermore, our bivariate analyses yielded strong evidence indicating that organizational justice has a more consistent relationship with the adherence to the code of silence across certain types of scenarios. We found that the organizational justice is the strongest and most consistent predictor of the adherence to the code of silence for police corruption scenarios. The effects on the organizational deviance scenarios and the interpersonal deviance scenarios are somewhat less consistent, while organizational justice was not linked with the adherence to the code of silence for the excessive force scenarios at all.

Not surprisingly, our multivariate analyses yielded a negative relationship between organizational justice and the respondents' own determination to adhere to the code of silence across the corruption scenarios. This negative relationship is significant for two of three corruption scenarios (i.e., gifts, theft from burglary). Our

Conclusion

analyses also yielded some interesting results. Organizational justice has stronger effects in the accepting free gifts scenario compared to the theft from the crime scene scenario. The limited effect of organizational justice in the theft from the crime scene scenario can be explained by the finding that the majority of the respondents are willing to report this type of misconduct.

We found no relationship between organizational justice and the respondents' willingness to report misconduct in the excessive force scenarios. While it is unclear why these two variables are unrelated, it can be argued that the effects of organizational justice may be masked by the politically sensitive nature of the police use of force in contemporary American society. Our results suggest a plausible interpretation that, in the present moment and historical context, organizational justice plays a secondary role in the excessive force scenarios.

Our multivariate analyses of the effects of organizational justice on respondents' own willingness to adhere to the code of silence in organizational deviance scenarios revealed an inconsistent relationship. While perceived organizational justice has a significant positive effect on the adherence to the code of silence in covering up a DUI crash scenario, it has a significant negative effect in the false overtime reporting scenario, and has no significant effect on the adherence to the code of silence in the false sick report scenario. Additional data are needed to explain why the relationship between the perceptions of organizational justice and respondents' decision to adhere to the code of silence varies so widely across organizational deviance scenarios.

Similarly, our multivariate analyses indicated that perceptions of organizational justice have inconsistent effects on the respondents' willingness to report misconduct in interpersonal deviance scenarios. While the effects of organizational justice on adherence to the code of silence are negative and insignificant in telling sexist jokes and yelling at coworkers scenarios, they are positive and significant in the spreading false rumors about a coworker scenario. This finding is unexpected because it would be reasonable to assume that officers should be more likely to report false rumors about a colleague when they believe that organizational justice exists in their agency, which is not the case here. Because some omitted factors, those not included in our multivariate models, may also affect the adherence to the code of silence, this puzzle will remain unanswered without additional data asking about officers' reasons for their decision.

Overall, our findings provide insight into what we know about the body of research on the code of silence. Police administrators could benefit from studying the effects of organizational justice on the adherence to the code of silence, and could more effectively tailor their policies and create a workplace where perceptions of organizational justice are promoted and the support for misconduct is reduced. Our findings also shed light on what we do not know and what needs to be examined in the future (e.g., the relationship between organizational justice and the respondents' decision to adhere to the code of silence across organizational deviance scenarios).

In the next chapter, we will examine the effects of self-legitimacy on police officers' prosocial and antisocial behaviors. Specifically, we will explore whether self-legitimacy can enhance the ability of the police integrity theory to explain officers' adherence to the code of silence. First, we will provide the theoretical explanations of the relationship between willingness to adhere to the code of silence and self-legitimacy. Then, we will present and discuss the results of bivariate and multivariate analyses that explain the correlation between these two measures.

References

Adams, J. S. (1965). Inequity in social exchange. *Advances in Experimental Social Psychology, 2*, 267–299.

Ambrose, M., & Schminke, M. (2009). The role of overall justice judgments in organizational justice research: A test of mediation. *Journal of Applied Psychology, 94*(2), 491–500.

Barclay, L. J., Skarlicki, D. P., & Pugh, S. D. (2005). Exploring the role of emotions in injustice perceptions and retaliation. *Journal of Applied Psychology, 90*(4), 629–643.

Bechtoldt, M., Welk, C., Zapf, D., & Hartig, J. (2007). Main and moderating effects of self control, organizational justice, and emotional labor on counterproductive behavior at work. *European Journal of Work and Organizational Psychology, 16*(4), 479–500.

Bradford, B., Quinton, P., Myhill, A., Porter, G., & G. (2014). Why do "the law" comply? Procedural justice, group identification and officer motivation in police organizations. *European Journal of Criminology, 11*(1), 110–131.

Byrne, D. (2005). Complexity, configurations and cases. *Theory, Culture & Society, 22*(5), 95–111.

Carless, D. (2006). Differing perceptions in the feedback process. *Studies in Higher Education, 31*(2), 219–233.

Cohen-Charash, Y., & Spector, P. (2001). The role of justice in organizations: A meta-analysis. *Organizational Behavior and Human Decision Processes, 86*(2), 278–321.

Colquitt, J. (2001). On the dimensionality of organizational justice: A construct validation of a measure. *Journal of Applied Psychology, 86*(3), 386–400. https://doi.org/10.1037/0021-9010.86.3.386

Colquitt, J. A., & Shaw, J. C. (2005). How should organizational justice be measured? In J. Greenberg & J. A. Colquitt (Eds.), *Handbook of organizational justice*. Lawrence Erlbaum Associates.

Colquitt, J. A., et al. (2001). Justice at the millennium: A meta-analytic review of 25 years of organisational justice research. *Journal of Applied Psychology, 86*(3), 425–445.

Colquitt, J., Noe, R., & Jackson, C. (2002). Justice in team: Antecedents and consequences of procedural justice climate. *Personnel Psychology, 55*(1), 83–109.

Colquitt, J. A., Scott, B. A., Judge, T. A., & Shaw, J. C. (2006). Justice and personality: Using integrative theories to derive moderators of justice effects. *Organisational Behaviour and Human Decision Processes, 100*(1), 110–127.

Crow, M. S., Lee, C., & Joo, J. (2012). Organizational justice and organizational commitment among South Korean police officers: An investigation of job satisfaction as a mediator. *Policing: An International Journal of Police Strategies & Management, 35*(2), 402–423.

De Angelis, J., & Kupchik, A. (2007). Citizen oversight, procedural justice, and officer perceptions of the complaint investigation process. *Policing: International Journal of Police Strategies & Management, 30*(4), 651–671.

Deutsch, M. (1975). Equity, equality, and need: What determines which value will be used as the basis of distributive justice? *Journal of Social Issues, 31*(3), 137–149.

Dick, G. P. (2011). The influence of managerial and job variables on organisational commitment in the police. *Public Administration, 89*(2), 557–576.

References

Donner, C., Maskaly, J., Fridell, L., & Jennings, W. (2015). Policing and procedural justice: A state-of-the-art review. *Policing: International Journal of Police Strategies & Management, 38*(1), 153–172.

Farmer, S., Beehr, T., & Love, K. (2003). Becoming an undercover police officer: A note on fairness perceptions, behavior, and attitudes. *Journal of Organizational Behavior, 24*(4), 373–387.

Fox, S., Spector, P. E., & Miles, D. (2001). Counterproductive work behavior (CWB) in response to job stressors and organizational justice: Some mediator and moderator tests for autonomy and emotions. *Journal of Vocational Behavior, 59*, 291–309.

Frear, K., Donsbach, J., Donsbach, J., Theilgard, N., Theilgard, N., Shanock, L., & Shanock, L. (2018). Supported supervisors are more supportive, but why? A multilevel study of mechanisms and outcomes. *Journal of Business and Psychology, 33*(1), 55–69.

Fridell, L. A., Maskaly, J., & Donner, C. M. (2020). The relationship between organizational justice and police officer attitudes toward misconduct. *Policing and Society*. https://doi.org/10.1080/10439463.2020.1834558

Haas, N. E., Van Craen, M., Skogan, W. G., & Fleitas, D. M. (2015). Explaining officer compliance: The importance of procedural justice and trust inside a police organization. *Criminology & Criminal Justice, 15*(4), 442–463.

Haberfield, M. R., & Kutnjak Ivković, S. (2015). *Measuring police integrity across the world: Studies from established democracies and countries in transition.* Springer.

Homans, G. (1961). The humanities and the social sciences: Joint concern with "individual" and values the arts distinct from social science distinctions of social status. *The American Behavioral Scientist, 4*(8), 3–6.

Kappeler, V. E., Sluder, R. D., & Alpert, G. P. (1998). *Forces of deviance: Understanding the dark side of policing.* Waveland Press.

Kutnjak Ivković, S., & Klockars, C. B. (1998). The code of silence and the Croatian police. In *Policing in central and Eastern Europe: Organizational, managerial, and human resource aspects* (College of police and security studies) (pp. 329–347).

Kutnjak Ivković, S., & Sauerman, A. (2016). Police integrity in South Africa: A tale of three police agency types. *Policing: International Journal of Police Strategies & Management, 39*(2), 268–283.

Kutnjak Ivković, S., & Shelley, T. O. (2010). The code of silence and disciplinary fairness: A comparison of Czech police supervisor and line officer views. *Policing: An International Journal of Police Strategies & Management, 33*(3), 548–574.

Kutnjak Ivković, S. Haberfeld, M.R., Cajner Mraović, I., Prpić, M.,* Hamm, J. A., & Wolfe, S. (2019). Seriousness of Police (Mis)Behavior and Organizational Justice. In Kutnjak Ivković, S. and M. Haberfeld (Eds.), Exploring Police Integrity: Novel Approaches to Police Integrity Theory and Methodology. New York: Springer.

Lersch, K. M. (2002). Are citizen complaints just another measure of officer productivity? An analysis of citizen complaints and officer activity measures. *Police Practice & Research, 3*(2), 135–147.

Leventhal, G. S. (1976). Advances in experimental social psychology. In Berkowitz & W. Walster (Eds.), *The distribution of rewards and resources in groups and organizations* (Vol. 9). Academic Press.

Leventhal, G. (1980). What should be done with equity theory?: New approaches to the study of fairness in social relationships. In *Social exchange* (pp. 27–55). Springer.

Leventhal, G. S., Karuza, J., & Fry, W. R. (1980). Beyond fairness: A theory of allocation preferences. *Justice and Social Interaction, 3*, 167–218.

Lim, V. K. (2002). The IT way of loafing on the job: Cyberloafing, neutralizing and organisational justice. *Journal of Organisational Behaviour, 23*(5), 675–694.

Lind, E., & Tyler, T. (1988). *The social psychology of procedural justice.* Springer.

McFarlin, D., & Sweeney, P. (1992). Distributive and procedural justice as predictors of satisfaction with personal and organizational outcomes. *Academy of Management Journal, 35*(3), 626–637.

Myhill, A., & Bradford, B. (2013). Overcoming cop culture? Organizational justice and police officers' attitudes toward the public. *Policing: International Journal of Police Strategies & Management, 36*(2), 338–356.

Palmiotto, M. J. (2001). Can police recruiting control police misconduct? In M. J. Palmiotto (Ed.), *Police misconduct: A reader for the 21st century* (pp. 344–354). Prentice Hall.

. (2015). President's task force on 21st century policing. In *Final report of the President's task force on 21st century policing*. COPS Office.

Reynolds, P., & Helfers, R. C. (2019). Organizational injustice and police misconduct: Predicting organizational defiance among police officers. *Criminology, Criminal Justice, Law, and Society, 20*(1), 53–70.

Rosenbaum, D., & McCarty, W. (2017). Organizational justice and officer "buy in" in American policing. *Policing: International Journal of Police Strategies & Management, 40*(1), 71–85.

Rothwell, G., & Baldwin, J. (2007). Whistle-blowing and the code of silence in police agencies: Policy and structural predictors. *Crime and Delinquency, 53*(4), 605–632.

Tankebe, J. (2010). Public confidence in the police: Testing the effects of experience of police corruption in Ghana. *British Journal of Criminology, 50*(2), 296–319.

Tankebe, J. (2014). Rightful authority: Exploring the structure of police self-legitimacy. *SSRN Electronic Journal*. https://doi.org/10.2139/ssrn.2499717

Tankebe, J., & Meško, G. (2014). Police self-legitimacy, use of force, and pro-organizational behavior in Slovenia. In G. Mesko & J. Tankebe (Eds.), *Trust and legitimacy in criminal justice* (pp. 261–277). Springer.

Thibaut, J. W., & Walker, L. (1975). *Procedural justice: A psychological analysis*. Lawrence Erlbaum Associates.

Thompson, B., & Daniel, L. G. (1996). Factor analytic evidence for the construct validity of scores: A historical overview and some guidelines. *Educational and Psychological Measurement, 56*(2), 197–208.

Truxillo, D., Bauer, T., Campion, M., & Paronto, M. (2002). Selection fairness information and applicant reactions: A longitudinal field study. *Journal of Applied Psychology, 87*(6), 1020–1031.

Tyler, T. R., Callahan, P. E., & Frost, J. (2007). Armed, and dangerous?: Motivating rule adherence among agents of social control. *Law & Society Review, 41*(2), 457–492.

Van Craen, C., & Skogan, W. G. (2017). Officer support for use of force policy: The role of fair supervision. *Criminal Justice and Behavior, 44*(6), 843–861.

Wolfe, S., & Lawson, S. (2020). The organizational justice effect among criminal justice employees: A meta-analysis. *Criminology, 58*(4), 619–644.

Wolfe, S., & Piquero, A. (2011). Organizational justice and police misconduct. *Criminal Justice and Behavior, 38*(4), 332–353.

Wolfe, S., Rojek, J., Manjarrez, V., & Rojek, A. (2018). Why does organizational justice matter? Uncertainty management among law enforcement officers. *Journal of Criminal Justice, 54*, 20–29.

Wu, G., & Maken, D. (2019). The Quagmire that is an Unwillingness to Report: Situating the Code of Silence Within the Chinese Police Context. *Criminal Justice and Behavior, 46*(4), 608–627.

Open Access This chapter is licensed under the terms of the Creative Commons Attribution 4.0 International License (http://creativecommons.org/licenses/by/4.0/), which permits use, sharing, adaptation, distribution and reproduction in any medium or format, as long as you give appropriate credit to the original author(s) and the source, provide a link to the Creative Commons license and indicate if changes were made.

The images or other third party material in this chapter are included in the chapter's Creative Commons license, unless indicated otherwise in a credit line to the material. If material is not included in the chapter's Creative Commons license and your intended use is not permitted by statutory regulation or exceeds the permitted use, you will need to obtain permission directly from the copyright holder.

Chapter 5
The Code of Silence and Self-Legitimacy

Abstract An emerging body of research suggests that the concept of self-legitimacy plays an important role in various outcomes associated with police officer attitudes and behaviors. In this chapter, we extend this literature by looking at the potential role that self-legitimacy may play in explaining the code of silence. The results suggest that self-legitimacy exerts an inconsistent effect on police officers' decisions to adhere to the code of silence across the scenarios. Moreover, adding self-legitimacy to the model does not substantively change the effect of the traditional police integrity variables. The chapter concludes with a discussion of theoretical and policy implications of these findings.

Keywords Police integrity · Police misconduct · Self-legitimacy · Police legitimacy · Police officers

Introduction

One of the key concerns in policing in recent years has been the legitimacy of the police. Typically, scholarly discussions of the legitimacy of the police revolve around how legitimate the community sees the police, or the so-called audience legitimacy (Bottoms & Tankebe, 2012). This strand follows from the work of Tyler (1990), which suggests that, when the public perceives an authority figure as legitimate, they are more likely to comply with law and cooperate with legal authorities. Weber (1978) also pointed out that there are multiple reasons why a person may comply with the commands from an authority beyond perceiving the authority as legitimate (e.g., self-interest, affinity for the authority).

However, this theoretical model may be incomplete, as it neglects to consider the claims of legitimacy that are made by those who are in power, the so-called self-legitimacy (Bottoms & Tankebe, 2012). The concept of self-legitimacy may play a role in enhancing the police integrity theory's ability to explain the officers' decisions to adhere to the code of silence, although—to our knowledge—this link has yet to be directly tested.

Lapses in integrity can certainly serve to erode the legitimacy of the police in the eyes of the public; however, a lack of self-legitimacy could also lead to lapses in integrity. The argument is that the degree of self-legitimacy an officer has, "…can serve to either promote or inhibit normatively desirable modes of policing" (Bradford & Quinton, 2014, p. 1023). In other words, the degree of self-legitimacy that an officer has may be associated with more desirable outcomes, as demonstrated in the empirical literature (see Gau & Paoline, 2021).

In this chapter, we explore the nature of the relationship between the code of silence and the officers' perceptions of their own power. In particular, we look at how officers' self-legitimacy influences their perceptions of (un)willingness to report misconduct. To do so, we use a two-step analytic process to estimate the effect of self-legitimacy on the code of silence. The first step focuses on the bivariate relationship between the code of silence and self-legitimacy. The second step of the analyses deploys multivariate models to test the effect of self-legitimacy—in addition to the traditional police integrity variables—on police officers' adherence to the code of silence.

Self-Legitimacy

Starting with the seminal work of Tyler (1990), criminologists have become increasingly interested in the concept of legitimacy. The initial formulation of the legitimacy model suggested that, when an authority figure is seen as legitimate by those over whom the power is exercised, they are more willing to voluntarily act in a manner that is consistent with what the authority figure would want (Tyler, 2003). In the realm of criminal justice, those who see the criminal justice system and its actors as legitimate are more willing voluntarily to obey the law and cooperate with officials. This is what is often called *audience legitimacy*.

Bottoms and Tankebe (2012) argue that, by only focusing on audience legitimacy, we are missing an important piece of the puzzle. Specifically, Bottoms and Tankebe (2012) suggest that legitimacy is a dialogue between the power holder and those over whom power is exerted. In other words, prior to considering the response from the audience, we must first consider the claim made by the authorities. Importantly, not all claims to power are legitimate. Legitimacy requires that the authority makes a legitimate claim to power in the form of an order, which can also be accepted by the audience (i.e., the person not in power; Raz, 2009).

The argument is distilled to suggest that legitimacy is both *dialogic* and *relational* (Bottoms & Tankebe, 2012). In short, legitimacy is predicated on a claim to a legitimate power made by an authority figure and the response from those over whom authority is exercised. Two important implications follow from this observation. First, legitimacy is not a fixed property, but rather something that is continually being negotiated between the authority figure and the audience. Second, as legitimacy is being constantly re-negotiated between the police and the public, the state of affairs also depends on how the police engaged in the re-negotiations and how they are perceiving their own authority. Hence, we may be missing important theoretical explanations for the behavior of police officers by omitting the self-legitimacy espoused by police officers.

The concept of self-legitimacy becomes even more important when considering the consequences of a lack of legitimacy. For most citizens, the police are the most visible and recognizable manifestations of the government's authority (Punch, 2000). As such, the police are the group that society—through the government—authorizes to use coercive means to bring people into behavioral compliance with societal expectations (Bittner, 1970). However, this is a proverbial double-edged sword. The less legitimate the public perceives the police to be, the more likely it becomes that the police will need to use coercive means to attain compliance (Muir, 1977). This increased use of coercion can then further erode the legitimacy of the police in the eyes of the public (Tyler, 1990). Some scholars have even gone so far as to argue that the need to use force is an indication that the authority has failed to make a legitimate claim in the eyes of the audience (Coicaud, 2002). In other words, officers who need to use force may already lack self-legitimacy, which further exacerbates the problem, thus creating a feedback loop.

The issue is further aggravated by the complex nature of the police role. The very nature of the police role makes it nearly impossible for the police to not use some sort of coercion to accomplish their social mandate (Bittner, 1970). Therefore, the simplistic nature of the feedback loop described above may be too reductionist. Instead, scholars argue that officers must learn to balance the complex moral mandate and the realities of their job (Muir, 1977). However, officers who are unable successfully to reconcile the competing demands may exhibit troubling behaviors (Tankebe, 2014; Tankebe & Meško, 2015).

The concept of self-legitimacy is further complicated by theoretical and operational ambiguity. Specifically, two theoretical arguments have been inconsistently tested in the criminological literature. The first argument that is grounded is the dialogic approach between the authority and the audience delineated by Bottoms and Tankebe (2012). In a nutshell, police self-legitimacy is formed as part of a dialogue with the public. The second version is based on the work of Barker (2001), which suggests that the feedback from the audience is irrelevant in the formation of an authority figures' self-legitimacy. As Bradford and Quinton (2014, p. 1028) argue, "police may gain legitimacy from the idea that they are different and apart from others in society…police have a legal duty, and are right, to enforce the law without 'fear or favor' irrespective of public approval." Essentially, the self-legitimacy of the police stems from the fact that officers feel they are entitled and empowered to take appropriate actions on behalf of the police. Some scholars argue that Barker's (2001) version is inappropriate to apply to the police because of the direct interaction between the police and the public, which augments the importance of the concept of audience legitimacy (Jonathan-Zamir & Harpaz, 2014).

Prior empirical work has conflated items that try to operationalize both theoretical approaches, which are based on two potentially conflicting theoretical arguments (Gau & Paoline, 2021). First, it is more difficult to determine what factors lead to self-legitimacy. These antecedents are largely important to ascertain which causal sequence of self-legitimacy is more appropriate. Second, the effects for the consequences of self-legitimacy are equally theoretically muddled. However, given the consistency in the research in this area (i.e., self-legitimacy exerts generally desirable effects), this may be less of a problem (see generally Gau and Paoline, 2021). Given the complexity of this issue and the focus of our book on another issue—the police code of silence—we make no attempt to refine the theoretical development of self-legitimacy. Instead, we focus our attention on how self-legitimacy may influence officers' decision to adhere to the code of silence.

Effects of Self-Legitimacy on Police Attitudes and Behavior

Beyond the purely scholarly study of the theoretical nature of self-legitimacy, it is important to consider what the potential effects of self-legitimacy are on the attitudes and behaviors of police officers. Research suggests that a person's identity (i.e., perception of self-legitimacy) will directly affect how they interpret and respond to situations (Archer, 2000). This observation led Bottoms and Tankebe (2012) to apply this approach to their study of police officers, arguing that an officer's self-legitimacy may influence how they interpret, evaluate, and respond to various situations.

Given that the police are authorized to use coercive force against the public and that their application restricts citizens' freedoms, research has disproportionately focused on the use of force decisions. Some of the earliest research in this area examined the relationship between the self-legitimacy and attitudes regarding the use of force among police officers in Ghana (Tankebe, 2014) and found no relationship between police officers' self-legitimacy and their general attitudes toward the legitimate use of force. It is important to note that these represented officers' global attitudes toward the use of force, which are notoriously problematic to measure because most participants impute information to respond to the question, which limits variability of responses (Roberts, 2003). Conversely, asking about specific attitudes typically results in better measurements (Cann et al., 1980; Hollin & Howells, 1987). Subsequent research looking at the relationship between self-legitimacy and the use of force addressed the methodological limitations of relying on global attitudes. Notably, Tankebe and Meško (2015) found that, in a sample of Slovenian police officers, self-legitimacy was associated with officers being less supportive of using force to resolve a hypothetical scenario instead of relying on a verbal warning. Taken together, these results suggest that police officers' self-legitimacy may be related to the tactics they are likely to employ when interacting with citizens.

A subsequent line of research suggests that self-legitimacy may also play an important role in the way officers treat community members. In their analysis of data from a police agency in the United Kingdom, Bradford and Quinton (2014) found that officers with higher self-legitimacy were more likely to espouse support for constitutional policing and preserving the rights of community members. These results imply that police officers with higher levels of self-legitimacy are less supportive of various police tactics that violate citizens' rights. Further, these data showed that self-legitimacy also reduced officers' support for the use of force against community members. The effect of self-legitimacy persisted even when controlling for officers' perceptions of organizational justice. The magnitude of the effect of self-legitimacy was the strongest for the support for procedurally just policing and preserving the rights of community members (Bradford & Quinton, 2014; see also Wolfe & Nix, 2017). A similar effect was found in research on Israeli police officers (Jonathan-Zamir & Harpaz, 2014).

The study of self-legitimacy has also been expanded to examine how self-legitimacy may insulate the police from deleterious media coverage in the wake of controversial police encounters with the public. In fact, Wolfe and Nix (2016) examined the role that self-legitimacy may play in explaining police officers' support for engaging in community partnerships after considering the so-called Ferguson effect (i.e., police officers' withdrawal from their official duties and responsibilities—to the extent possible—in response to the additional public scrutiny caused by widely publicized police killings and other police actions). The results from this study show that self-legitimacy mediated the Ferguson effect on officers' willingness to engage in community partnerships. This finding is particularly salient in light of simultaneous consideration of the Ferguson effect and self-legitimacy. The Ferguson effect represents an erosion—or at least strong questioning—of legitimacy of the police (i.e., audience legitimacy) caused by their publicized actions. The fact that self-legitimacy mediates this relationship is consistent with Barker's (2001) argument about the formation of self-legitimacy.

Self-Legitimacy and the Code of Silence

Empirical evidence suggests the importance of self-legitimacy in predicting certain prosocial and antisocial behaviors of officers (e.g., Bradford & Quinton, 2014; Jonathan-Zamir & Harpaz, 2014; Wolfe & Nix, 2017). At the same time, we found no empirical studies linking self-legitimacy and adherence to the code of silence. However, there are strong theoretical reasons to suppose that self-legitimacy may be associated with the (un)willingness to report colleagues' misconduct. To make the link between these two constructs, one must understand police integrity theory and the theoretical mechanisms that are posited to explain self-legitimacy.

There are four dimensions of the police integrity theory (Klockars et al., 2000, 2006). A more comprehensive description of the theory is presented in Chap. 1, so we outline an abbreviated version here. The first dimension focuses on *organizational* rules and the degree to which police officers understand and support the official rules (Klockars et al., 2000, 2006). The second dimension of the police integrity theory focuses on various *organizational control mechanisms* and emphasizes the police agency's internal disciplinary system (Klockars et al., 2000, 2006). The third dimension is the *cultural* dimension, which explores the respondents' (un) willingness to report misconduct and their assessments of peers' willingness to do the same. The fourth dimension of the police integrity theory explores the influence of the *larger social context* on police integrity, the dimension that has been the least tested of the four (Kutnjak Ivković, 2015; Maskàly et al., 2019).

The way the four dimensions of police integrity theory connect to self-legitimacy comes from the dialogic approach that officers use to form self-legitimacy. Specifically, Wolfe and Nix (2017) suggest that interactions with three groups of people are particularly important for self-legitimacy: supervisors, colleagues, and the public. These groups could be connected to the four dimensions identified by the police integrity theory. Specifically, the interactions with supervisors are part of the organizational rules and organizational control mechanism dimensions. Interaction with peers is akin to the cultural element posited by the police integrity theory. Finally, the conversation with the public that is key to Bottoms and Tankebe's (2012) model of self-legitimacy could be part and parcel of the larger social context in which the police operate—the fourth dimension of the police integrity theory.

There clearly is some conceptual overlap between the police integrity theory and self-legitimacy. One of the key arguments proffered by Bottoms and Tankebe (2012) is that self-legitimacy is directly tied to the moral rectitude of the power vested in the authority. This suggests that, if officers lacking self-legitimacy may also have a compromised moral compass, this flaw may then affect their willingness to report their peers' rule-violating behavior (i.e., traditional police misconduct). Conversely, those with more self-legitimacy may have a moral compass that is so attuned to the larger goals of policing that an officer may fail to report misconduct because it achieves a larger goal (i.e., noble cause corruption). However, scholars have argued that those with the greatest degree of self-legitimacy will not conflate the means and the ends in their decision-making processes (Archer, 2000). In other words, an officer who truly has self-legitimacy would still be willing to report a colleague who engaged in misconduct that was aimed at accomplishing some higher goal.

The police integrity theory and self-legitimacy are logically congruent. Agencies are trying to balance the competing concerns of deterring officers' behavior with appropriately severe discipline without increasing officers' feelings of organizational injustice (Fridell et al., 2021). Research finds that self-legitimacy mediates the effect of organizational (in)justice (i.e., how organizational rules are implemented). In other words, self-legitimacy can serve as a protective factor in police agencies with a weak organizational inclination toward police integrity. Yet, we are unaware of any study that has directly tested the relationship between self-legitimacy and the theory of police integrity.

This Chapter

Extant research indicates that self-legitimacy has the capacity to predict certain pro-social and antisocial behaviors of officers. Yet, although there are strong theoretical reasons to assume that self-legitimacy and the (un)willingness to report colleagues' misconduct could be related, we found no empirical study linking self-legitimacy and the adherence to the code of silence. The purpose of this chapter is to fill the gap in the extant literature by determining whether self-legitimacy can enhance the ability of the police integrity theory to explain officers' adherence to the code of silence (i.e., unwillingness to report). We expand the traditional police integrity literature by also considering the effect of self-legitimacy on the police officers' adherence to the code of silence. Furthermore, we explore the relationship on a range of forms of police misconduct, from police corruption and the use of excessive force, to organizational and interpersonal deviance.

Methodology

Sample

In 2018/2019, we administered a survey to a sample of 148 police officers from a medium-sized municipal police agency from the United States. For full characteristics of the sample and the data collection procedures, please see Chaps. 1 and 2.

Measures

The analyses in this chapter examine the effects of self-legitimacy on the respondents' expressed (un)willingness to report misconduct. The measures of police integrity, which include the code of silence, came from the newest version of the police integrity questionnaire (Kutnjak Ivković et al., 2019) that includes 12 different scenarios that depict instances of police corruption, use of excessive force, organizational deviance, and interpersonal deviance. After being presented with the scenarios, participants were asked to respond to the same seven questions for each of the scenarios. Participants indicated their own perceptions of seriousness, how serious their colleagues would perceive the described action to be, whether the action was a violation of organizational rules, what the expected discipline would be, what they think the appropriate level of discipline should be, their own willingness to report the misconduct, and their peers' willingness to report the misconduct. For additional details, please see Chaps. 1 and 2.

Dependent Variable

The dependent variable for the analyses in this chapter is the respondents' *own expression of adherence to the code of silence* for misconduct depicted in each scenario. Initially, participants responded on a 5-point Likert scale, which ranged from

1 ("definitely would not report") to 5 ("definitely would report"). The code of silence variable was created by coding the responses from the officers who expressed a general unwillingness to report the actions (i.e., 1 or 2 on the original scale) as a 1, and the responses from the officers who expressed a general willingness to report (i.e., 3–5 on the original scale) as a 0.

Organizational Independent Variables

We have also included several organizational variables previously identified by the police integrity theory research. These variables include the participants' *own perceptions of seriousness*, whether the conduct *violates organizational rules*, assessments of the *expected discipline* imposed by the police agency, and estimates of *most police officers' willingness to report*. For a more detailed description, see Chaps. 1 and 2.

Self-Legitimacy Independent Variables

The questionnaire that was administered to the officers contained several additional items, including two items that measured the concept of *self-legitimacy*. Because of the theoretical ambiguity of the construct described above, measurement of self-legitimacy has been inconsistent in the research (Gau & Paoline, 2021). To make the results more easily comparable to those of other studies, we used items from Wolfe and colleagues' (2018) study.

The specific items and their descriptive statistics are presented in Table 5.1. For each of these items, respondents indicated their level of agreement using a traditional 5-point Likert scale. The items were subjected to principal axis factoring to look for evidence of internal validity. The results of the analysis show that both items load together on a single construct, both with high factor loading coefficients ($\lambda = 0.80$; Table 5.1). Additionally, measures of internal consistency showed that the items have an acceptable degree of reliability ($\alpha = 0.84$). Based on the evidence, we then estimated factor scores for the self-legitimacy factor. This self-legitimacy variable was then used in subsequent analyses.

Table 5.1 Measurement properties of self-legitimacy items

Self-legitimacy items ($\alpha = 0.84$)	M (SD)	λ
I have confidence in the authority vested in me as a police officer	4.33 (1.14)	0.80
I understand how my work directly contributes to the success of my agency	4.38 (1.05)	0.80

Analytic Strategy

As in prior chapters, the analyses proceed in two stages. In the first stage of the analyses, we examine the bivariate relationship between the willingness to adhere to the code of silence and self-legitimacy for each of the 12 scenarios. These analyses are a series of point-biserial correlations between willingness to adhere to the code of silence and the self-legitimacy scores. The second stage of the analyses focuses, for each of the 12 scenarios, on the multivariate relationship between the willingness to adhere to the code of silence and self-legitimacy. Again, we employed the cross-folded LASSO technique for making out of sample inferences using the same controls as in prior chapters. For additional information on this technique, please see Chap. 2.

Results

The Effects of Self-Legitimacy on the Code of Silence

We first analyzed the bivariate relationship between the willingness to report the misconduct and the latent measure of self-legitimacy. The results (Table 5.2) generally indicate that the relationship is negative and statistically significant. It is significant for all scenarios apart from the scenario of interpersonal deviance depicting an officer spreading false rumors about a coworker. The average size of the correlation coefficient for interpersonal deviance scenarios—like this one—is the strongest across the four types of misconduct. In fact, the average size of the correlation is the strongest for interpersonal deviance, followed by organizational deviance, then use of excessive force, while it is the weakest for corruption. In fact, the average correlation between self-legitimacy and the code of silence for the corruption scenarios is 24% less than for the interpersonal deviance scenarios.

There is a fair degree of heterogeneity in the effects for the scenarios *within* the four sub-types of misconduct (Table 5.2). A closer examination does not show a consistent pattern in the strength of these relationships. In other words, for example, we do not find systematic evidence that self-legitimacy exerts a stronger effect on the more serious scenarios within each subtype.

The Effects of Self-Legitimacy and Police Integrity on to the Code of Silence

The results are shown in Table 5.3. Overall, the traditional police integrity variables do not substantively change with the inclusion of the self-legitimacy items. There are some minor differences in the results (i.e., changes in the magnitude of

Table 5.2 Bi-variate relationship between self-legitimacy and the code of silence

	ρ	Average ρ value by scenario type
Corruption		−0.19
Accepting gifts	−0.21*	
Theft from burglary scene	−0.19*	
Doing supervisor errands	−0.16*	
Excessive use of force		−0.20
Shooting suspect in back	−0.15*	
Verbally abusing citizen	−0.28*	
Supervisor fails to stop beating	−0.16*	
Organizational deviance		−0.23
Covering up DUI crash	−0.24*	
False sick report	−0.26*	
False overtime reporting	−0.18*	
Interpersonal deviance		−0.25
Telling sexist jokes	−0.39*	
Yelling at coworkers	−0.24*	
False rumors about coworker	−0.11	

Note: * = $p < 0.05$

coefficients) and a few changes in the substantive interpretation of the variables, most of which are attributed to the stabilized standard errors after the inclusion of the self-legitimacy measure. We comment briefly on the differences in the results presented in the unconditional models shown in Chap. 2.

Police Corruption

The first set of models (Table 5.3) shows the multivariate results for the corruption scenarios. The results here indicate that self-legitimacy exerts an inconsistent effect on the willingness to adhere to the code of silence for the three corruption scenarios. In the scenario in which the officer accepts gifts from members of the community, the effect of self-legitimacy is negative (OR = 0.75, $p < 0.05$), which is consistent with the bivariate relationship estimated above. However, for the other two scenarios, increased self-legitimacy is associated with a greater likelihood of adhering to the code of silence (i.e., being unwilling to report misconduct). It is unclear what could account for these differences, both of which are contrary to their respective bivariate relationships. Finally, the effect of self-legitimacy on the adherence to the code of silence is the strongest—marginally—for the most serious corruption scenario (i.e., theft from a burglary scene).

Results 87

Table 5.3 Self-legitimacy effects on the code of silence

	Corruption			Excessive force		
	Gifts	Theft from burglary	Supervisor errands	Shooting suspect in the back	Verbally abusing citizen	Failing to report beating
Self-legitimacy	0.75*	1.88***	1.84***	3.30*	1.24*	0.74***
Others' code of silence	11.95***	62.24***	111.89***	227.42***	93.40***	162.53***
Violation of policy	0.39***	–	0.60***	0.08***	0.34***	1.06
Own perceptions of seriousness	0.37***	–	0.74*	0.01***	0.29***	0.06***
No discipline[a]	2.57***	13.36***	2.08***	0.01***	2.06***	0.64
Dismissal[a]	1.45	0.99	3.07***	0.41	10.81***	2.77**
χ^2 (df)	396.60 (6)	208.43 (4)	349.92 (6)	97.76 (6)	305.84 (6)	309.03 (6)
	Organizational deviance			Interpersonal deviance		
	Covering up DUI crash	False sick report	False overtime reporting	Telling sexist jokes	Yelling at coworkers	Spreading false rumors about coworker
Self-legitimacy	0.73***	1.02	0.73***	0.98	0.44***	1.03
Others' code of silence	37.61***	92.03***	86.34***	56.43***	47.76***	42.45***
Violation of policy	0.70***	0.74	2.44***	1.19	2.37***	0.37***
Own perceptions of seriousness	0.21***	0.12***	0.05***	0.29***	0.10***	0.71***
No discipline[a]	0.65	27.99***	1.26	2.99***	3.44***	2.41***
Dismissal[a]	0.86	0.25***	1.70	1.88	1.36	8.48***
χ^2 (df)	321.26 (6)	151.89 (6)	273.97 (6)	269.51 (6)	417.24 (6)	200.78 (6)

Notes: * = $p < 0.05$, ** = $p < 0.01$, *** = $p < 0.001$; – parameter excluded due to collinearity
[a]Reference category is "intermediate discipline."

The results from the more traditional police integrity measures largely remain unchanged with the inclusion of these new variables, with the estimates of other police officers' willingness to adhere to the code of silence being the strongest predictor of the police officers' own adherence to the code. We see that the effects for all the variables for the scenario of accepting free gifts are only marginally attenuated compared to the unconditional models presented in Chap. 2. The same is largely true for the scenario depicting supervisory corruption as well. The key change for this scenario is that the own perceptions of seriousness, not significant in the unconditional model, become significant after the inclusion of self-legitimacy, which stabilized the standard errors for this variable in the updated model. In this model, the more serious police officers evaluated the scenarios, the less likely they were to say that they would adhere to the code of silence.

The biggest differences are seen in regard to the other officers' willingness to report the misconduct in the theft scenario and the supervisory errands scenario. There, the coefficients for the type of discipline expected are slightly attenuated (as in the other scenarios), but the substantive conclusion remains unchanged. However, after including self-legitimacy in the model, the effect of other officers' adhering to the code of silence is augmented by 41.8% for theft from a crime scene and 29.3% for the supervisory corruption scenario. These increases suggest that the inclusion of the self-legitimacy item may be explaining common variation with the measure of the respondent's peers' willingness to adhere to the code of silence.

Use of Excessive Force

Next, we turn to the results for the scenarios depicting the excessive use of force scenarios (Table 5.3). Again, the self-legitimacy measure performs inconsistently, this time across the excessive force scenarios. There is a strong positive effect of self-legitimacy on adherence to the code of silence for the scenario depicting an officer shooting a suspect in the back (OR = 3.30, $p < 0.05$) and, to a lesser degree, for the scenario depicting verbal abuse of a citizen (OR = 1.24, $p < 0.05$). Both of these findings contravene the theoretical expectations of self-legitimacy. However, the effect is theoretically consistent for the scenario depicting a failure to report a beating (OR = 0.74, $p < 0.001$).

The results for the traditional police integrity variables largely remain unchanged—substantively and in magnitude—across the three scenarios, with the exception of others' willingness to report. The magnitude of these coefficients here is larger for each of the three excessive force scenarios than it is in the unconditional models presented in Chap. 2. In fact, after including self-legitimacy, the effect of peers' adherence to the code of silence is strengthened by 31.7% compared to the unconditional model. Similarly, the effect is augmented by 20.4% for the scenario of failing to stop a beating and 9.8% for the verbal abuse of a citizen. Again, this would suggest that the inclusion of self-legitimacy into these models largely adds unique explanatory power to the model, although there is a pattern developing in the self-legitimacy item for these excessive force scenarios—and those with corruption: officers' perceptions of their peers' willingness to report seems to be related to their level of self-legitimacy. Given that conversations—and relationships—with peers is theoretically one of the accomplishments officers need to have to establish self-legitimacy (Wolfe & Nix, 2017), this is not entirely surprising.

Organizational Deviance

Next, we turn to the multivariate results for the organizational deviance scenarios (Table 5.3). For these scenarios, self-legitimacy performs more consistently across scenarios. In fact, self-legitimacy exerts the same magnitude of effect for covering up a DUI crash of a fellow officer and for false overtime reporting (OR = 0.73, $p < 0.001$). However, there is no significant effect for the scenario depicting an officer calling in sick to work. Indeed, self-legitimacy exerts an effect for the two more serious scenarios, but not the least serious of the three.

The effects from the traditional police integrity variables remain substantively unchanged with the inclusion of self-legitimacy. Thus, while self-legitimacy may be associated with the willingness to report misconduct in some instances of organizational deviance, the effect here is unique to those exerted by the other police integrity variables. The unique nature of self-legitimacy in these organizational deviance scenarios is distinct from those of police integrity variables, suggesting that self-legitimacy may influence officers' decision-making processes differently based on the type of misconduct that is encountered. The organization—or at least supervisors—has been identified as a key partner in the dialogue to develop self-legitimacy (Wolfe & Nix, 2017). The results here may suggest that officers' dialogue with the organization in the formation of self-legitimacy is seen as different for instances of misconduct against the organization relative to those outside the organization—as is the case in most of the corruption and excessive force scenarios.

Interpersonal Deviance

Finally, we look at the effect of self-legitimacy on interpersonal deviance (Table 5.3). Self-legitimacy only exerts a significant negative effect on the scenario in which an officer rudely yells at his/her coworkers for a perceived slight (OR = 0.44, $p < 0.001$) and does not exert a significant effect on the other two interpersonal deviance scenarios. Unlike other types of scenarios which show a trend in the effect but are not statistically significant (largely because of the size of the standard errors), this is not the case with the other two interpersonal deviance scenarios. In fact, the effects here are substantively null.

Furthermore, we see that the results associated with the traditional police integrity measures again largely remain unchanged. For example, the effects for the police integrity variables are almost identical for the telling sexist jokes scenario and the scenario involving spreading false rumors about coworkers. There are a few differences for the scenario depicting the officer rudely yelling at his/her coworkers. The only exception to this trend is again seen in the effect of other officers' adherence to the code of silence for the yelling at coworkers scenario, where the effect is augmented by 98.9% compared to the unconditional model presented in Chap. 2. This is the only scenario in which self-legitimacy exerts a significant effect. Therefore, it is not entirely surprising that this effect changes consistently with prior scenarios in which self-legitimacy exerts a significant effect. Again, this finding is suggesting that the conversations with peers may indeed be an important component in the formation of self-legitimacy—or vice versa.

Conclusion

In this chapter, we have added a scale of self-legitimacy to the multivariate model of the code of silence. As it turns out, the addition of self-legitimacy measures left the traditional police integrity variables largely unchanged, except for magnifying the effect of others' willingness to report.

The results from this set of analyses show a complicated relationship between the code of silence and self-legitimacy. For three scenarios, the relationship is positive and significant (i.e., self-legitimacy *increases* the adherence to the code of silence), in five scenarios it is negative and significant (i.e., self-legitimacy *decreases* the adherence to the code of silence), and in the remaining four there is a null effect (i.e., self-legitimacy is *not related* to the code of silence).

To further tease out the nature of this complex relationship between the code of silence and self-legitimacy, we looked at systematic patterns across the scenarios. There does not seem to be an apparent relationship between the type of misconduct depicted in the scenario (i.e., corruption, use of excessive force, organizational deviance, and interpersonal deviance) and the nature of the effect that self-legitimacy has on the code of silence (i.e., positive or negative). Similarly, self-legitimacy is not related in any systematic way to the seriousness of misconduct protected by the code.

We have also tried to assess whether the nature of the questions we asked about self-legitimacy was related to our results. Extant literature has developed two distinct theoretical causal frameworks for the development of self-legitimacy. The first theoretical framework involves the dialogic approach outlined by Bottoms and Tankebe (2012), whereby self-legitimacy is a conversation that officers have with various constituencies in the development of their self-legitimacy. Following this approach, self-legitimacy is highly dependent upon the feedback from others, be they supervisors, peers, or community members. The second theoretical framework, proposed by Barker (2001), suggests that self-legitimacy is unilaterally determined by the officer's feelings and sentiments and is not influenced by how the police officer is perceived by others. These two theoretical models have led to a bifurcation in the literature about how self-legitimacy should be measured and captured, with some research identifying different antecedents of each of these forms of self-legitimacy (Gau & Paoline, 2021).

The measure of self-legitimacy that we used in this study was comprised of only two items, one of which (i.e., "I understand how my work directly contributes to the success of my agency") tapped the dimension specified by the dialogic approach specified by Bottoms and Tankebe (2012), while the other (i.e., "I have confidence in the authority vested in me as a police officer") is more consistent with Barker's (2001) approach. The nature of the questions asked to measure self-legitimacy makes it difficult to disentangle the theoretical puzzle surrounding self-legitimacy in our study. In unreported sensitivity analyses, we examined the independent effect of each of these two variables measuring self-legitimacy on the code of silence. As it turns out, the results were substantively unchanged. In other words, while the magnitude of the effects was different across these two variables, the substantive conclusions (i.e., self-legitimacy increases or decreases adherence to the code of silence) were the same. This suggests that, while it remains important to resolve the theoretical ambiguity surrounding the development of self-legitimacy, resolving it would not make the interpretation of the results easier in this study.

The fact that the results from this study are somewhat inconsistent with the emerging body of literature may have also stem from organizational differences. Research consistently points to the fact that police agencies vary in terms of their culture (Cordner, 2017) and their level of integrity (Klockars et al., 2000, 2006). These differences are often driven by different organizational emphases and policies, both of which could affect the operationalization of self-legitimacy. Specifically, officers in the agencies that put more emphasis on constitutional policing and police integrity could have different perceptions of what self-legitimacy is than the police officers from agencies focused on more aggressive and questionable tactics of crime control. On the one hand, for police officers from police agencies of high integrity, the concept of self-legitimacy could rely on the view that their role is to serve the community and engage in a dialogue with the community about how policing should be done. On the other hand, for police officers from the police agencies willing to engage in more aggressive and questionable tactics, the concept of self-legitimacy could incorporate the view that their role is very traditional, focused primarily on aggressive law enforcement.

While these are theoretical possibilities—including a full range of other views of self-legitimacy between these two extremes—there is nothing that we can specifically articulate about the agency from which these data were collected that may shine a light on this differentiation. However, the agency that participated in our study is not known as being particularly progressive or innovative (i.e., actively reinforcing the importance of constitutional policing) nor is it known for being particularly regressive in any domain (i.e., consistently failing to control police misconduct). Instead, this agency is more akin to a typical police agency in the United States.

The importance of this characterization comes into play when considering the other police agencies included in extant self-legitimacy research. Policing scholars have consistently identified a "big city bias" in the study of policing, suggesting that the largest police agencies in the United States are both routinely more progressive and more likely to be studied (Falcone et al., 2002). Furthermore, research suggests that many police departments refuse to participate in the research concerning topics considered to be particularly sensitive (Archbold & Maguire, 2002). Taken together, this may suggest that prior self-legitimacy research may have been conducted in large agencies that were more willing to participate in research and were more progressive than the mid-size agency that agreed to participate in our study. It is difficult to confirm our speculation because many police agencies that participate in research are anonymized—as is our agency—as a condition of their participation.

The implication is that, perhaps, the definition of self-legitimacy utilized by police officers from the agencies that agreed to participate in prior research could be quite different from the definition of self-legitimacy used by police officers in the agency that agreed to participate in our study. This would suggest that, while self-legitimacy may indeed be an important factor in the decision-making process and formation of officers' attitudes, what it means to have self-legitimacy may be understood differently by police officers from different agencies. This is a key question for subsequent research that focuses on self-legitimacy, especially studies linking self-legitimacy and police integrity research.

In our next, at the same time final chapter, we continue our exploration of the factors that affect the police officers' code of silence. We argue that, to detect the full effect of each factor, such exploration should incorporate these different types of factors simultaneously. After presenting the theoretical arguments for the connections between these factors, we present the results from the full models that seek to explain police officers' decision to adhere to the code of silence using the traditional police integrity variables, perceptions of disciplinary fairness, organizational justice, and self-legitimacy.

References

Archbold, C. A., & Maguire, E. R. (2002). Studying civil suits against the police: A serendipitous finding of sample selection bias. *Police Quarterly, 5*, 222–249.
Archer, M. S. (2000). *Being human: The problem of agency*. Cambridge University Press.
Barker, R. (2001). *Legitimating identities: The self-presentations of rulers and subjects*. Cambridge University Press.
Bittner, E. (1970). *The functions of the police in modern society*. National Institute of Mental Health.
Bottoms, E. A., & Tankebe, J. (2012). Beyond procedural justice: A dialogic approach to legitimacy in criminal justice. *Journal of Criminal Law and Criminology, 102*, 119–170.
Bradford, B., & Quinton, P. (2014). Self-legitimacy, police culture and support for democratic policing in an English constabulary. *British Journal of Criminology, 54*, 1023–1046.
Cann, A., Calhoun, L. G., & Selby, J. W. (1980). Attributions for delinquent behavior: Impact on consequences and consistency information. *British Journal of Social and Clinical Psychology, 19*, 33–40.
Coicaud, J. M. (2002). *Legitimacy and politics: A contribution to the study of the political right and responsibility* (trans. D.A. Curtis). Cambridge University Press.
Cordner, G. (2017). Police culture: Individual and organizational differences in police officer perspectives. *Policing: An International Journal, 40*, 11–25.
Falcone, D., Wells, L. E., & Weisheit, R. A. (2002). The small town department. *Policing: An International Journal of Strategies and Management, 25*, 371–384.
Fridell, L. A., Maskály, J., & Donner, C. M. (2021). *The relationship between organizational justice and police officer attitudes toward misconduct*. Policing and Society. Forthcoming. https://doi.org/10.1080/10439463.2020.1834558.
Gau, J. M., & Paoline, E. A. (2021). Police officers' self-assessed legitimacy: A theoretical extension and empirical test. *Justice Quarterly, 38*, 276–301.
Hollin, C. R., & Howells, K. (1987). Lay explanations of delinquency: Global or offense-specific? *British Journal of Social Psychology, 26*, 203–210.

References

Jonathan-Zamir, T., & Harpaz, A. (2014). Police understanding of the foundations of their legitimacy in the eyes of the public: The case of commanding officers in the Israel National Police. *British Journal of Criminology, 54*, 469–489.

Klockars, C. B., Kutnjak Ivković, S., Harver, W. E., & Haberfeld, M. R. (2000). *The measurement of police integrity, NIJ research in brief*. National Institute of Justice.

Klockars, C. B., Kutnjak Ivković, S., & Haberfeld, M. R. (2006). *Enhancing police integrity*. Springer.

Kutnjak Ivković, S. (2015). Studying police integrity. In S. Kutnjak Ivković & M. Haberfeld (Eds.), *Measuring police integrity across the world*. Springer.

Kutnjak Ivković, S., Haberfeld, M. R., & Peacock, R. (2019). Overlapping shades of blue: Exploring police officer, supervisor, and administrator cultures of police integrity. In S. Kutnjak Ivković & M. Haberfeld (Eds.), *Exploring police integrity: Novel approaches to police integrity theory and methodology*. Springer.

Maskály, J., Kutnjak Ivković, S., Haberfeld, M., Donner, C., Chen, T., & Meyers, M. (2019). Assessing the validity of police integrity scale in a comparative context. *Policing and Society, 30*(6), 618–638.

Muir, W. K. (1977). *Police: Streetcorner politicians*. University of Chicago Press.

Punch, M. (2000). Police corruption and its prevention. *European Journal of Criminal Policy and Research, 8*, 301–324.

Raz, J. (2009). *The Authority of Law: Essays on Law and Morality*. New York: Oxford University Press.

Roberts, J. V. (2003). Public opinion and mandatory sentencing: A review of international findings. *Criminal Justice and Behavior, 30*, 483–508.

Tankebe, J. (2014). Rightful authority: Exploring the structure of police self-legitimacy. *SSRN Electronic Journal*. https://doi.org/10.2139/ssrn.2499717

Tankebe, J., & Meško, G. (2015). Police self-legitimacy, use of force, and pro-organizational behavior in Slovenia. In G. Meško & J. Tankebe (Eds.), *Trust and legitimacy in criminal justice* (pp. 261–277). Springer.

Tyler, T. (1990). *Why people obey the law*. Yale University Press.

Tyler, T. (2003). Procedural justice, legitimacy, and the effective rule of law. *Crime & Justice, 30*, 283–357.

Weber, M. (1978). *Economy and Society: An Outline of Interpretive Sociology*. Berkeley, CA: University of California Press.

Wolfe, S. E., & Nix, J. (2016). The alleged "Ferguson effect" and police willingness to engage in community partnerships. *Law and Human Behavior, 40*, 1–10.

Wolfe, S. E., & Nix, J. (2017). Police officers' trust in their agency: Does self-legitimacy protect against supervisor procedural injustice? *Criminal Justice and Behavior, 44*, 717–4732.

Open Access This chapter is licensed under the terms of the Creative Commons Attribution 4.0 International License (http://creativecommons.org/licenses/by/4.0/), which permits use, sharing, adaptation, distribution and reproduction in any medium or format, as long as you give appropriate credit to the original author(s) and the source, provide a link to the Creative Commons license and indicate if changes were made.

The images or other third party material in this chapter are included in the chapter's Creative Commons license, unless indicated otherwise in a credit line to the material. If material is not included in the chapter's Creative Commons license and your intended use is not permitted by statutory regulation or exceeds the permitted use, you will need to obtain permission directly from the copyright holder.

Chapter 6
Lessons Learned About the Code of Silence

Abstract This chapter discusses the findings of a case study of a mid-size U.S. police agency in the context of extant research and elaborates on the lessons learned from our study. Based on the empirical study of the contours of the code of silence across behaviors that violate tenets of police integrity, including police corruption, use of excessive force, interpersonal deviance, and organizational deviance, the chapter illustrates the interconnectedness between the code of silence and the police agency's organizational perspectives. The study emphasizes the role that the police officers' organizational attitudes play in their willingness to adhere to the code of silence, from their perceptions of how willing other police officers are to report misconduct and the severity of the disciplinary threat that their police agency is making, to their perceptions of self-legitimacy and organizational justice. The chapter concludes the book by offering a discussion of theoretical and policy implications of the findings.

Keywords Police integrity · Organizational justice · Distributive fairness · Self-legitimacy · Code of silence

Introduction

The code of silence has been a topic of scholarly work since the 1970s (e.g., Bittner, 1970; Klockars et al., 2000, 2004, 2006; Westley, 1970). Since the 1990s, the theory of police integrity and the related methodology have been used to measure empirically the contours of the code of silence across the world (for an overview, see Kutnjak Ivković, 2015; see also Klockars et al., 2004; Kutnjak Ivković & Haberfeld, 2015, 2019). Extant research on police integrity has established that police integrity measures, such as perceptions of misconduct seriousness, views about expected discipline, and the anticipated peers' willingness to report misconduct, are strongly related to the police officers' (un)willingness to stick to the code of silence (see

Chap. 2). We have also demonstrated that the perceptions of disciplinary fairness seem to affect the respondents' determination whether to report misconduct (see Chap. 3). In further extension of police integrity work, we have incorporated measures of organizational justice (see Chap. 4) and self-legitimacy (see Chap. 5) to assess their relationship with the code of silence, while controlling for the police integrity measures. Up to this point, we have not yet combined these different approaches to obtain a full model of factors that affect the code of silence. Such an approach would allow us to evaluate the complexity of the ways in which these factors relate to the code of silence and to assess their individual strength in this multivariate space.

During multivariate statistics courses, most students are repeatedly told some form of the adage that "we do live in a multivariate world." This comment is meant to imbue future analysts with the belief that there is often more than a singular explanation for the same behavior, especially in the social sciences. After all, human behavior is thought to be infinitely complex. However, this realization—and analytic consequences—of this adage must be weighed against the competing concern for parsimonious theoretical explanations. In fact, students are often taught that parsimony is one of the criteria under which a criminological explanation can be judged (Akers & Sellers, 2013). This means that in our quest to explain any phenomenon and develop theoretical models, we must balance the competing concerns of completeness and parsimony.

Essentially, scholars are trying to balance these competing concerns. Neglecting important variables in a theoretical explanation may be inadvertently causing two problems. First, by ignoring key variables from the model we may end up identifying a spurious relationship between two variables that are in fact caused by another common factor, which is often excluded from the model (Weisburd et al., 2016). This error has at least two consequences. For scholars, this may lead to unnecessarily squandered research efforts to identify theoretical explanations of behavior. For practitioners, it could result in the wrong factors being manipulated to control the behavior in question. In other words, as it relates to the topic of this book, such an approach could result in policing scholars focusing on inappropriate factors to explain why officers adhere to the code of silence and can lead police executives to manipulate the wrong factors to control this behavior. Both outcomes are deeply problematic for police integrity research, which is difficult enough to begin with (e.g., Klockars et al., 2004; 2006).

The second problem associated with trying to balance the multivariate world and the parsimonious theoretical explanations is related to the concept of omitted variable bias. The problem of omitted variable bias, an issue frequently neglected in much of the criminological research (Weisburd et al., 2016), speaks to the fact that omitting an important explanatory variable from a regression model may yield problematic parameter estimates (Weisburd, 2010). Specifically, if a key variable that is correlated with the dependent variable (i.e., adhering to the code of silence) is omitted from the model, it could make the results of the entire model highly questionable, especially when correlated with another independent variable in the model (Angrist and Pischke, 2008). Failing to include the appropriate variables in our theoretical explanations of social behavior can be deeply problematic.

In short, this means that our explanations of the factors affecting the code of silence explored in this book *so far* may have been incomplete. Our primary argument here is that, while police integrity theory, which has been rigorously and robustly tested (Klockars et al., 2006; Maskàly et al., 2019), offers one type of explanation for the officer's decision to adhere to the code of silence, the theoretical argument could potentially be furthered with the inclusion of other factors. In prior chapters, we have looked at perceptions of disciplinary fairness (Chap. 3), organizational justice (Chap. 4), and self-legitimacy (Chap. 5) and their link with the police offices' adherence to the code of silence. However, each of these factors was independently added to the traditional police integrity variables in prior chapters and, as the discussion on omitted variable bias above suggests, the results from prior models may present an incomplete explanation of an officer's decision to adhere to the code of silence. This is an especially pressing concern given the potentially strong theoretical and empirical relationships between the factors that were independently added in prior chapters.

In this chapter, we briefly explain the links between these additional theoretical concepts (i.e., discipline fairness, organizational justice, self-legitimacy) and the traditional police integrity measures (i.e., perceptions of policy violation, other police officers' willingness to report, and perceptions of seriousness). We start by drawing together the traditions of disciplinary fairness and organizational justice. We continue by connecting the theoretical link between organizational justice and self-legitimacy. While the concepts of disciplinary fairness and self-legitimacy are almost certainly related, given that disciplinary fairness falls under the umbrella of organizational justice, to our knowledge the link has never been expressly tested nor theoretical linkages previously established. After presenting the theoretical arguments for the connections, we present the results from the full models that attempt to explain police officers' decision to adhere to the code of silence using the traditional police integrity variables, perceptions of disciplinary fairness, organizational justice, and self-legitimacy.

Disciplinary Fairness and Organizational Justice

One of the recurrent arguments in philosophy and social scientific literature revolves around the related concepts of fairness and justice, which tend to be indiscriminately used interchangeably (Colquitt et al., 2005). Humans living in social settings have long been overly concerned about being treated fairly by other members in the social group. Furthermore, this idea of fair treatment has several subdomains, which are frequently encapsulated under the larger umbrella of organizational justice, comprised of distributive, procedural, and interpersonal justice (Greenberg, 1987).

The first type of justice was distributive justice, which can be traced back to the writings of ancient Greek philosophers (e.g., Plato). The primary argument of distributive justice is that people are concerned with the fairness of various types of outcomes (Adams, 1963). Initially, much of the work in this area emphasized that individuals are concerned about receiving their fair share of outcomes, rewards, and promotions. There have been many iterations of distributive justice theories, but one of the common elements is that perceptions of distributive justice are not as much predicated on the absolute level of the outcome as they are on the relative comparisons to what is known about the outcomes that others in the same social group are receiving (Festinger, 1954).

Initial conceptualizations of distributive justice focused on the distribution of rewards, but research soon recognized that punishments—or discipline—generate the same pattern of concerns (Colquitt et al., 2005). Essentially, people may be willing to accept punishment for engaging in certain types of behavior, although they want to make sure that the distribution of this punishment is fair. There are three potential concerns: equity, equality, and need (Deutsch, 1975). The concept of *equity* is based on the initial construction of distributive justice, that a person receives a fair outcome based on their contribution (Adams, 1963, 1965). The concept of *equality* focuses on the fact that all people who do the same thing will receive the same distribution (Deutsch, 1985). This is akin to the concept of proportionality in criminal punishments, whereby all similarly situated defendants will be punished in the same way for the same crime (Feeley, 1978). The final concept—*need*—is the least developed of three concepts. It focuses on what sorts of aggravating and mitigating factors a person may have that affect his/her distribution (Lerner, 1977). Determining which of these specific motivations is present in the current data is beyond the scope of this book. Instead, we use this to highlight the link between organizational justice and disciplinary fairness.

Obviously, there is a direct link between organizational justice and discipline fairness through the lens of distributive justice, but the theoretical links between these two concepts do not stop there. Instead, the issue is more nuanced when looking at the literature on effective discipline in organizations, which suggests that the amount of discipline administered may be an important factor for the way employees feel about their organizations (Arvey & Ivancevich, 1980). If the discipline is too harsh, it may have unintended consequences because members of the organization become afraid of the discipline, rather than seeing discipline as a tool to enhance learning (Parke, 1972). Furthermore, employees are concerned that the organization consistently disciplines all employees for the same behaviors (Gary, 1971), which, in turn, enhances the effectiveness of discipline. The same effect is seen for individual managers consistently disciplining their subordinates (Rosen and Jardee, 1974). Finally, we see that employees tend to be concerned with the fact that all managers will issue the same type of discipline for the same types of behaviors to their subordinates (Walster and Walster, 1975). Each of these concerns can be lumped together under the umbrella of distributive justice, as each of them represents employee concerns that the discipline reflects equity and equality. There are also concerns of need that have been identified in the literature, although the implications and consequences are not nearly as fleshed out in the extant empirical research.

Additionally, research suggests the nature of the relationship to the person administering the punishment/discipline is also an important factor in determining how effective punishment/discipline can be. Specifically, discipline tends to be best received when there is a relatively close relationship between the person administering the discipline and the person being disciplined (Parke, 1972). Essentially, this type of situation leads the person who made the mistake to feel the discipline more acutely because of the positive relationship with the person delving out the discipline. This speaks to the concept of interactional justice within organizations, whereby the disciplined person is more likely to feel that they were treated with dignity and respect while being disciplined (Greenberg, 2009).

Finally, the process through which discipline is meted out also has important effects. Specifically, research suggests that conveying trustworthy motives in the form of a rationale for the punishment is particularly effective in enhancing the efficacy and perceived fairness of punishment (Parke, 1972). This is particularly true when there is a substantial gap in time between the behavior and the discipline (Aronfreed, 1965). This concept can easily be applied to policing, given the often-substantial amount of time that it takes to conduct internal investigations related to lapses in police integrity. Again, the procedure in which the rationale for punishment is clearly outlined demonstrates to the employee being punished that the punishment is being implemented for trustworthy reasons. This is a key element of procedural justice, the final subcomponent of organizational justice.

Organizational Justice and Self-Legitimacy

The theoretical relationship between organizational justice and self-legitimacy has been fleshed out relatively recently. Bradford and Quinton (2014, p. 1023) succinctly identify the nature of the relationship by stating, "…organizational configurations—officers' sense of their place in their organization and the relationships they have with both it and external stakeholders—can serve to promote or inhibit normative modes of policing." Self-legitimacy is a concern in policing because of the dialogic conversation between power holders and those over whom they exert their power (Bottoms & Tankebe, 2012). An officer's sense of self-legitimacy is important because it has been shown to explain differences in officer behavior and attitudes (e.g., Bradford & Quinton, 2014; Tankebe & Meško, 2015). Therefore, self-legitimacy may play an important role in explaining police integrity (see Chap. 5).

Relatively little is known about how self-legitimacy is developed. Tankebe (2014, p. 5) stated that "direct interactions with others provide information about confidence in self-legitimacy," but did not define who precisely the others are. Nix and Wolfe (2017) suggest that these conversations may be conducted with at least three primary groups: supervisors, colleagues, and the public. Our interest here revolves around the effects of those conversations that officers are having with their supervisors, specifically the organizationally just nature of those conversations. The theoretical argument suggests that officers' self-legitimacy may be eroded or otherwise inhibited from forming in organizations that lack organizational justice.

The theoretical antecedents to self-legitimacy have been sparsely tested, although the limited evidence suggests organizational justice—and its components—are generally positively associated with self-legitimacy. For example, Nix and Wolfe (2017) found that perceptions of organizational justice are positively associated with self-legitimacy, even after considering the effects of negative publicity. This implies that, while certain types of negative publicity can certainly erode the self-legitimacy of officers, this effect can be relatively easily overcome by enhancing the perceptions of organizational justice within the organization. Moreto et al. (2021) found a similar effect for conservation rangers' feelings of self-legitimacy. Moreover, Meško et al. (2017) also found that tenets of organizational justice affect the self-legitimacy of prison officers in Slovenia, where perceptions of self-legitimacy were associated with better treatment of inmates. This emerging body of literature suggests that organizational justice plays a role in shaping police officers' self-legitimacy, although no scholarship of which we are aware directly links self-legitimacy and organizational justice to police integrity.

When considering the relationship between organizational justice and self-legitimacy, an open question revolves around the theoretical specification and operationalization of these concepts. There seems to be measurement ambiguity associated with both organizational justice and self-legitimacy, but for different reasons. The trouble with organizational justice stems from the potential theoretical redundancy of organizational justice with other measures, namely organizational commitment. Some scholars argue that the relationship between organizational justice and other factors is mediated by organizational commitment (Cohen-Charash and Spector, 2001). This may suggest that the effects ascribed to organizational justice may, in fact, truly belong to organizational commitment. Bradford and Quinton (2014) found that organizational identity—an analogous indicator to organizational commitment—mediated the relationship between procedurally fair treatment from supervisors and self-legitimacy. Research shows that the effect of organizational justice and a measure of police integrity (i.e., perceptions of seriousness) were partially mediated by organizational commitment (Fridell et al., 2021).

The second open theoretical and methodological problem revolves around the ambiguous theoretical operationalization of self-legitimacy. As Gau and Paoline (2020) point out, there have been two distinct discussions on the role of self-legitimacy: one that is inwardly focused and the other that involves public perceptions. The inward-focused theoretical notion of self-legitimacy puts the focus on the holder's assessment of their legitimacy, regardless of other factors (Barker, 2001). Conversely, the externally focused theoretical notion of self-legitimacy says that an officer's claim of self-legitimacy involves an ongoing dialogue with the public (Tankebe, 2010). This distinction is important because, as Gau and Paoline (2020) show, measures of organizational justice exert differential effects. Notably, the scholars include two pseudo-measures of organizational justice analogous to organizational justice measures that are targeted at the officer's direct supervisors and the organization's top management. The results from Gau and Paoline's study (2020) show that officers' self-legitimacy is positively related, although not significantly, to supervisory support, and negatively and significantly related to top management support, whereas the opposite effects, although with the same significance interpretation, are observed for externally generated self-legitimacy. Furthermore, there was no significant bivariate relationship between the two measures of self-legitimacy. Taken as a whole, this would suggest that the relationship between organizational justice and self-legitimacy—if any—may be highly dependent upon the operational definition of self-legitimacy and the operational definition of organizational justice.

Disciplinary Fairness and Self-Legitimacy

The link between disciplinary fairness and self-legitimacy is arguably the most theoretically underdeveloped among the independent variables in this book. However, there are at least two reasons to suspect that there might be a theoretical relationship between these two concepts. The first is the transitive property of logic. This property states that, if A → B and B → C, then A → C. Thus, as shown above, because disciplinary fairness is related to organizational justice and organizational justice is related to self-legitimacy, it follows that self-legitimacy should also be related to disciplinary fairness. At the same time, the extant literature does not provide enough evidence to perform a robust literature review on the topic. Instead, we offer some early evidence that seeks preliminarily to tie these two constructs together.

We argue that the link between self-legitimacy and disciplinary fairness can be found by examining the operational definitions of each. Another definition of self-legitimacy is "power-holders' recognition of, or confidence in, their own individual entitlement to power" (Tankebe, 2014, p. 3). Some scholars argue that officers with a higher degree of self-legitimacy are better able to perform their duties because they do not fear being unfairly disciplined for their actions (Nix and Wolfe, 2017), which is the key for linking this concept with disciplinary fairness.

Research finds that overly harsh punishments can have a paralyzing effect on the decision-making and learning of employees in organizations (Parke, 1972). This would suggest that, when police organizations harshly discipline officers who make mistakes, there may be an unintended consequence in the form of eroding officers' self-legitimacy such that they no longer have confidence in the power bestowed upon them. Conversely, other research suggests that, when discipline is too lenient, this can also have deleterious effects because such discipline likely fails to change or stop the adverse behaviors (Weinstein, 1969). This failure to change behaviors and attitudes could then expose the disciplined officers to adverse treatment by their peers. An officer's peers represent one of the three constituencies with whom the officer engages in the dialogic conversation to build self-legitimacy. Therefore, discipline that is too harsh may lead to the officers' erosion of self-legitimacy because the officers feel that they are unqualified/incapable of holding the power vested in them. On the other hand, discipline that is too lenient may lead to the officer's peers questioning the officer's legitimacy as a police officer. Therefore, there is indeed a relationship between self-legitimacy and disciplinary fairness, although the precise connection could use additional theoretical refinement and empirical assessment.

This Chapter

Police integrity theory has a storied and consistent ability to explain adherence to the code of silence around the world. In this chapter, we seek to determine whether the inclusion of several theoretically relevant factors adds explanatory power to the traditional police integrity variables. Specifically, we investigate whether simultaneous addition of measures of disciplinary fairness, organizational justice, and self-legitimacy changes our ability to predict police officers' adherence to the code of silence in the scenarios depicting instances of various types of misconduct. Since each of these other constructs—especially organizational justice and self-legitimacy—have been used by policing scholars previously, they have proven to be quite successful in explaining various facets of police officers' attitudes and behaviors, but there were no direct tests of their effectiveness in explaining police integrity. In prior chapters, we have seen how each of these factors operates independently when added to the traditional police integrity variables. Given the strong theoretical links between each of these additional constructs, it is possible that failing to include all of them in the same model may lead to omitted variable bias.

Methodology

Sample

In late 2018/2019, we surveyed police officers from a medium-sized municipal police agency in the United States. The sample consists of 148 officers that serve as sworn police officers in this agency. For a more detailed description of the sampling method and sample characteristics, please see Chaps. 1 and 2.

Measures

As with previous chapters, we are interested in explaining police officers' decisions to adhere to the code of silence using traditional police integrity variables and the other independent variables described in previous chapters (Chaps. 3, 4, and 5). All measures were included in the newest version of the police integrity questionnaire designed by Kutnjak Ivkovicć and colleagues (2019). The central focus of the police integrity questionnaire are 12 scenarios depicting four categories of police misconduct: police corruption, use of excessive force, organizational deviance, and interpersonal deviance—each represented by three scenarios (see Chap. 2). For more details, please see Chaps. 1 and 2.

Methodology

Dependent Variable

Our measure of the respondents' adherence to the code of silence is based on their *own willingness to report* misconduct described in each scenario. Respondents were asked to indicate their willingness to report the behavior using a 5-point Likert scale that ranged from 1 (definitely would not report) to 5 (definitely would report). Given that we are interested in adherence to the code of silence (i.e., unwillingness to report), we collapsed the answers into two categories, with values of 1 and 2 coded as 1 (i.e., adhere to the code of silence) and the remaining values coded as 0. There are two exceptions to this rule for two of the most serious scenarios (i.e., theft from a burglary scene and shooting a suspect in the back), where reporting was much more ubiquitous than for other scenarios. In these cases, we assigned a value of 1 to those who initially indicated 1 through 3 on the initial Likert scale, with the other two values (4 and 5) coded as 0. For additional details, please see Chap. 2.

Organizational Independent Variables

We incorporated several traditional police integrity variables into multivariate models. They include police officers' own *estimates of misconduct seriousness*, their evaluations of misconduct as a *violation of official rules*, their views about what the *appropriate discipline* is and what the *expected discipline* would be, and their estimates of how willing *other police officers* in their agency would be *to report misconduct*. For details, please see Chap. 2.

Disciplinary Fairness Independent Variables

In addition to the above variables, we have included a measure of *disciplinary fairness*. For details, please see Chap. 3.

Organizational Justice Independent Variables

The multivariate models of the respondents' adherence to the code of silence include the global measure of *organizational justice*. For details, please see Chap. 4.

Self-Legitimacy Independent Variables[1]

The models that we have developed incorporate two measures of *self-legitimacy*. The results of the factor analysis showed that they are loading together as a simple construct of self-legitimacy. For details, please see Chap. 5.

---

[1] The results here indicate that there is a strong positive correlation between organizational justice and self-legitimacy ($\rho = 0.71$, $p < 0.05$), consistent with the theoretical linkage. Alternative analy-

Individual Independent Variables

The models also include several measures of the respondents' demographic characteristics: *length of service, gender, assignment, supervisory status,* and *education.* We utilize these demographic characteristics as the control variables. For details, please see Chap. 2.

Analytic Strategy

The analyses build on the multivariate models of the code of silence presented in prior chapters. We predict adherence to the code of silence for all 12 scenarios using the traditional police integrity variables, the measure of disciplinary fairness, the measure of organizational justice, and the measure of self-legitimacy. We group together the results by misconduct type (i.e., corruption, use of excessive force, organizational deviance, and interpersonal deviance). Again, we continue to use the LASSO modeling procedure to estimate the multivariate effects, net of the control variables. For details, please see Chap. 2.

Results

The Effects of Police Integrity, Distributive Fairness, Organizational Justice, and Self-Legitimacy on the Code of Silence

Police Corruption

After including all independent variables in the model (Table 6.1), we see that the effects of the traditional police integrity measures (e.g., others' adherence to the code of silence, violation of agency rules, perceptions of seriousness) are largely consistent with the results from prior research. In all scenarios, officers who feel their colleagues are unlikely to report the misconduct are also more likely to say that they would adhere to the code of silence. Additionally, knowledge of organizational rules (violation of policy) and perceptions of seriousness are both negatively associated with adherence to the code of silence, again consistent with prior research.

---

ses using the general linear model were employed to look for potential multicollinearity issues for the organizational justice and self-legitimacy measures. These analyses showed that the variance inflation factor (VIF) value was less than 2.5 for each for each model. Across all 12 scenarios the average VIF for organizational justice was 2.44 and for self-legitimacy was 2.31. All of this suggests that, while the two constructs are highly correlated, including both in the same model does not appear to lead to problematic collinearity (Thompson et al., 2017).

Furthermore, compared to the respondents who expected some intermediate discipline, the respondents who expected no discipline tended to be more likely to say that they would not report (Table 6.1). Finally, compared to the respondents who expected intermediate discipline, the respondents who expected dismissal were more likely to say that they would adhere to the code of silence in two out of three scenarios than the respondents who expected intermediate discipline (Table 6.1).

Comparing the results of the traditional police integrity variables to those from the unconditional models estimated in Chap. 2, the results are substantively the same. Some of the effect sizes were attenuated by the inclusion of all the independent variables in the model, although some of the effects strengthened, especially in the scenario depicting supervisory corruption. Overall, these results suggest that the addition of these new variables is not redundant with the traditional police integrity variables and that they enhance the explanation of the police officers' adherence to the code of silence.

The effects of disciplinary fairness remain substantively the same as they did in Chap. 3. However, the inclusion of the additional independent variables leads to harsh discipline—relative to a fair discipline—being statistically significant for the scenario of accepting free gifts (OR = 0.49, $p < 0.01$), unlike the models estimated in Chap. 3. The same pattern is observed for the same variable in the supervisory corruption scenario (OR = 0.45, $p < 0.01$). This would suggest that, while disciplinary fairness may be theoretically related to organizational justice—especially the distributive justice subcomponent—this construct offers a unique addition to our ability to explain adherence to the code of silence.

A very different pattern is seen for organizational justice in these corruption scenarios. After including the other independent variables, we see that organizational justice significantly reduces the likelihood that officers would adhere to the code of silence in each of these three scenarios. These results are similar to the results from Chap. 4, although the effects are now significant for all scenarios. This consistent organizational justice effect is in accordance with theoretical expectations and prior research.

Finally, the results for self-legitimacy universally show that officers who have a higher sense of self-legitimacy are more likely to adhere to the code of silence in these corruption scenarios, net of all of the other factors. This is consistent with the results from the unconditional models of self-legitimacy presented in Chap. 5. However, compared to the results reported in Chap. 5, the effects in current models have been substantially strengthened for two of the scenarios (i.e., theft from a burglary scene and supervisory corruption) and reversed for the scenario depicting an officer accepting free gifts. Given the strength of the relationship between self-legitimacy and the other independent variables, such a stark change in the effect size is not surprising. This is the embodiment of the problems associated with omitted variable bias. These results challenge the emerging lore surrounding the importance of officers developing self-legitimacy.

Table 6.1 Full model estimates of adherence to the code of silence

	Corruption			Excessive force		
	Gifts	Theft from burglary	Supervisor errands	Shooting suspect in the back	Verbally abusing citizen	Failing to report beating
Lenient punishment [a]	0.37***	0.85	0.11***	0.02***	1.30	0.66
Harsh punishment [a]	0.49**	8.66***	0.45**	0.30	36.33***	4.48***
Organizational justice	0.27***	0.21***	0.30***	1.33	0.60**	1.37***
Self-legitimacy	1.90**	12.36***	5.56***	4.27	1.61**	0.54***
Others' code of silence	12.22***	23.75***	40.29***	61.17***	43.51***	19.26***
Violation of policy	–	–	0.53**	0.04***	0.27***	1.61
Own perceptions of seriousness	0.29***	–	0.52***	0.01**	0.42***	0.04***
No discipline [b]	2.12***	1.92	4.85***	0.01***	4.93***	1.02
Dismissal [b]	2.93***	0.14***	14.17***	0.22*	4.30***	2.73
χ^2 (df)	468.15 (9)	180.52 (7)	249.68 (9)	89.04 (9)	349.67 (9)	285.16 (9)
	Organizational deviance			Interpersonal deviance		
	Covering up DUI crash	False sick report	False overtime reporting	Telling sexist jokes	Yelling at coworkers	Spreading false rumors about coworker
Lenient punishment [a]	0.51	0.09***	1.06	0.30***	0.06***	0.71
Harsh punishment [a]	1.27	3.59***	2.62**	4.11***	25.58***	0.47
Organizational justice	2.31***	0.80	0.43***	0.63***	2.77***	2.86***
Self-legitimacy	0.30***	1.67*	1.63*	1.58*	0.11***	0.40***
Others' code of silence	35.44***	–	76.73***	61.40***	58.18***	27.66***
Violation of policy	0.79	0.72	2.20***	0.92	2.67***	0.32***
Own perceptions of seriousness	0.21***	0.07***	0.04***	0.29***	0.11***	0.73**
No discipline [b]	0.88	12.57***	1.03	3.09***	21.58***	2.23***
Dismissal [b]	1.08	0.11***	0.68	3.42	6.71***	11.20*
χ^2 (df)	394.07 (9)	417.92 (8)	246.79 (9)	262.62 (9)	152.75 (9)	144.40 (9)

w: * = $p < 0.05$, ** = $p < 0.01$, *** = $p < 0.001$, – = parameters excluded due to collinearity
[a]Reference category is fair discipline
[b]Reference category is intermediate discipline

Results   107

Use of Excessive Force

The results from the full models for the three scenarios depicting the use of excessive force (Table 6.1) show that the traditional police integrity variables are again consistent with prior research and largely remain substantively unchanged relative to the results from the unconditional models presented in Chap. 2. The only substantive changes are the changes in the effect of the type of discipline that an officer who engaged in this type of behavior would likely receive. The interpretation of the effects remains substantively unchanged in this full model, and the difference in the statistical significance of these two variables is largely attributable to the standard errors becoming more stable with the inclusion of the additional independent variables. In other words, the inclusion of these independent variables accounted for some amount of noise in the estimates of the traditional police integrity variables, especially as related to the expected type of discipline. The same is also true for the results assessing the effect of the measures of disciplinary fairness in these excessive force scenarios.

We now turn to the results from the measure of organizational justice. Although in Chap. 4 organizational justice was not significantly associated with adherence to the code of silence in the excessive force scenarios, a more complex pattern of the effect of organizational justice emerges after other independent variables are included in the multivariate models. Specifically, for these scenarios depicting the use of excessive force, organizational justice increases adherence to the code of silence (failing to report a beating; OR = 1.37, $p < 0.001$), reduces adherence to the code of silence (verbally abusing motorist; OR = 0.60, $p < 0.01$), and exerts no significant effect (shooting suspect in the back; OR = 1.33, $p > 0.05$). It is unclear what drives these differential effects here, although the two scenarios where organizational justice is positively associated with adherence to the code of silence—regardless of whether the effect is significant—involve the use of physical force, and the other scenario does not.

Likewise, we see a complex set of findings emerge for self-legitimacy. In Chap. 5, the effects of self-legitimacy on the code of silence were complicated. This pattern of findings repeats itself here. Just like organizational justice, self-legitimacy increases the likelihood of adhering to the code of silence in one scenario (verbally abusing a motorist; OR = 1.61, $p < 0.01$), reduces the likelihood in one scenario (failing to report a beating; OR = 0.54, $p < 0.001$), and has no significant effect on the third (OR = 4.27, $p > 0.05$).

Organizational Deviance

The effects of the traditional police integrity variables in the organizational deviance scenarios (Table 6.1) are largely consistent with prior police integrity research. Furthermore, apart from reducing the effect sizes, the results are substantively similar to those presented in Chap. 2. Again, this suggests that the independent variables are adding a unique explanatory power to the model, rather than being redundant with the police integrity theory variables.

Next, we turn to perceptions of disciplinary fairness for each of these three scenarios. The results here are substantively identical to those presented in Chap. 3. The key differences are seen in the reduction in the magnitude of the effect for each of these variables after the inclusion of the other independent variables. This would suggest that there is some redundancy with the disciplinary fairness and the other independent variables included in the model. The potential redundancy here is not entirely surprising, given the theoretical and empirical relationship between the constructs. A potential explanation for this effect may stem from the effects of organizational justice. Organizational justice is theoretically and—to varying degrees—empirically associated with disciplinary fairness. Including both variables in the model can lead to some redundancy in the estimates, which seems to be the case here. In the full models, the effects of organizational justice are strengthened compared to the results in Chap. 4, and the interpretation of the effects remains substantively unchanged. These results suggest that there is some shared variance between disciplinary fairness and organizational justice, although not as much as might be expected.

Conversely, the results from self-legitimacy are quite different from the results presented in Chap. 5. In the models with only self-legitimacy and traditional police integrity measures, we see either a null or negative effect of self-legitimacy on the adherence to the code of silence (see Chap. 5). However, with the inclusion of the other independent variables, the pattern of findings becomes more complex. We see that self-legitimacy reduces the likelihood that an officer would adhere to the code of silence in covering a DUI crash of a fellow officer (OR = 0.30, $p < 0.001$), but significantly increases adherence to the code of silence in the other two scenarios: falsely calling in sick (OR = 1.67, $p < 0.05$) and falsely reporting overtime (OR = 1.63, $p < 0.05$).

Interpersonal Deviance

Finally, we look at the results for the interpersonal deviance scenarios (Table 6.1). Again, the results from the traditional police integrity variables presented here are substantively identical to those presented in the unconditional models in Chap. 2. The same is true for the disciplinary fairness measures. Again, this would suggest that both the traditional police integrity variables and the disciplinary fairness measures exert independent effects on the adherence to the code of silence in these interpersonal deviance scenarios.

We notice some differences when examining the effect of perceptions of organizational justice in these interpersonal deviance scenarios. The results from Chap. 4, which only added organizational justice and traditional police integrity measures to the model, show that organizational justice is only associated with increased adherence to the code of silence for the scenario depicting the spreading of false rumors about a coworker (OR = 1.50, $p < 0.001$). However, after including all of the independent variables in this chapter, the size of this effect has nearly doubled (OR = 2.86, $p < 0.001$). Additionally, we see that, unlike in Chap. 4, organizational justice now exerts significant—although differential—effects on adherence to the code of silence for the scenario depicting the telling of sexist jokes (OR = 0.63, $p < 0.001$) and the scenario depicting yelling at coworkers (OR = 2.77, $p < 0.001$).

Again, it is not entirely clear what is different about these scenarios that causes the differential effects of organizational justice. However, these varying results may suggest that officers are not simply "pencil whipping" the survey, and instead are making independent judgments about each scenario. This contention seems to be supported by the pattern of results for self-legitimacy, which shows substantively opposite effects compared to organizational justice in these scenarios. In other words, when organizational justice increases adherence to the code of silence, self-legitimacy reduces it. Finally, again, we note that the inclusion of the other independent variables reduced the noise in the parameter estimates for self-legitimacy, a largely expected outcome in light of the theoretical and conceptual overlap of these constructs.

Conclusion

Because of the police agencies' semi-military organization, the code of silence has developed in each police agency as part of police culture to protect police officers (e.g., Bittner, 1970; Klockars et al., 2000). As Westley (1970) and Bittner (1970) hypothesized, police recruits are socialized into police culture—both at the police academy and during their field training—and taught that they can rely only on their fellow officers. One mechanism used to acquire this trust is adhering to the code of silence and, hence, protecting police misconduct committed by their fellow officers.

Therefore, it comes as no surprise that the empirical analyses in this book (e.g., Chap. 2) reveal the presence of the code of silence among the police officers in the police agency we study. Specifically, for every scenario, including the most serious ones (i.e., stealing from a crime scene, abusing deadly force), there is a certain number of police officers who said that they would not report misconduct. With the exception of these two scenarios, at least one out of five police officers, if not more, said that they would not report *any* type of misconduct described in our study. In fact, in some scenarios, such as accepting gratuities, verbally abusing citizens, or covering up DUI crash, the *majority* of the police officers in our study seemed to be willing to adhere to the code of silence.

As various independent commissions (e.g., Knapp Commission, 1972; Mollen Commission, 1994) demonstrate, the code of silence—tolerance of police misconduct without reporting it—is a serious obstacle in the efforts to curtail police misconduct. Whereas assessing the contours of the code of silence is a critical step in such efforts (e.g., Klockars et al., 2000; 2004; Kutnjak Ivković & Haberfeld, 2015, 2019), it is not the only step. The goal of this book has been to determine the factors associated with the strong code of silence and offer evidence-based approach to curtailing the code of silence and, ultimately, police misconduct.

The results of our full models confirm the strong effect of the traditional police integrity measures (e.g., others' adherence to the code of silence, violation of agency rules, perceptions of seriousness) on the police officers' decision to adhere to the code of silence. To begin with, we found the effects of police culture at play; in all 12 scenarios, officers who assessed that their colleagues would not report police misconduct are also more likely to say that they would not report either. The perceptions of police culture tolerant of police misconduct have the strongest and most consistent effect on the respondents' own expressed willingness to adhere to the code of silence. This finding, aligned with the extant literature (Hickman et al., 2016; Kutnjak Ivković et al., 2018, 2019; Long et al., 2013; Lim & Sloan, 2016; Peacock et al., 2020; Van Droogenbroeck et al., 2019), demonstrates the important effect that the police culture has on the way police officers think about police misconduct. Police administrators interested in curtailing the code of silence should learn how accurate the police officers' perceptions of their peer culture are. If police officers' views indicate overconfidence in their peers' willingness to adhere to the code, police administrators should share with police officers the more accurate view of their peer culture. On the other hand, if police officers are accurately "reading" their peers' willingness to not report, then the more challenging task that the administrators have is to change the peer culture by conveying an unambiguous message about the importance of official rules and their consistent enforcement, as well as by providing the rewards for reporting.

This research shows that the more serious police officers view police misconduct, the less likely they are to adhere to the code of silence. The result is strong and consistent across different forms of police misconduct. This strong negative relationship between the expressed willingness to adhere to the code of silence and perceptions of misconduct seriousness persists even in the presence of other potential factors, such as perceptions of organizational justice or self-legitimacy. These results fit the large body of extant police integrity literature (Cheloukhine et al., 2015; Haberfeld, 2004; Hickman et al., 2016; Khechumyan & Kutnjak Ivković, 2015; Klockars et al., 1997, 2004, 2006; Kutnjak Ivković et al., 2013, 2016, 2018, 2019; Kutnjak Ivković & Khechymian, 2013; Kutnjak Ivković & Sauerman, 2013; Lobnikar & Meško, 2015; Long et al., 2013; Lim & Sloan, 2016; Maskàly et al., 2019; Pagon & Lobnikar, 2000; Peacock et al., 2020; Porter & Prenzler, 2016; Vallmüür, 2015; Westmarland, 2006; Wu & Makin, 2019). They also open another avenue for police administrators willing to curtail the code of silence. Specifically, police officers should be (re)taught to view police misconduct as a serious matter. Nevertheless, police administrators should follow up and demonstrate—through the enforcement of official rules and administration of discipline for their violations—that they perceive police misconduct as a serious matter as well.

Conclusion

How serious police misconduct is evaluated typically has been closely tied with the assumption that misconduct violates official rules and that discipline would result in such rule violations (e.g., Klockars et al., 2000, 2004, 2006; Kutnjak Ivković & Haberfeld, 2015, 2019). In about one-half of the scenarios, our full models do not link the knowledge that police misconduct described in the scenarios violates official rules with the respondents' expressed willingness to adhere to the code of silence. On the other hand, in most scenarios in which the relationship is statistically significant, there is a clear negative relationship between the respondents' recognition that the behavior violates official rules and their willingness to stick to the code of silence. These findings demonstrate the importance of establishing clear official rules prohibiting misconduct (e.g., Klockars et al., 2000, 2006).

However, establishing the official rules is a necessary, but not a sufficient condition. Even the most carefully designed official rules need to be enforced consistently and fairly to be effective. Severity of expected discipline (or the lack of any discipline) is also related to how willing police officers are to report misconduct. Our findings show that, compared to the respondents who expected some intermediate discipline, the respondents who expected no discipline tended to be more likely to say that they would not report misconduct. When the police officers perceive that the police administration will not mete out any discipline or will mete out only very mild discipline in the form of a verbal reprimand, these police officers would be more likely to say that they would not report such misconduct—why bother if there will be no discipline at all? Assuming that the police officers accurately predict what the expected discipline will be, the message for police administrators is very clear: if particular behavior is defined as police misconduct, then the administration should mete out discipline in all the cases in which police officers engage in such rule-violating behavior. On the other hand, if the police officers are underestimating the severity of the disciplinary threat that the police administration is actually making, then the administrators need to teach police officers what the accurate disciplinary threat is.

The situation with dismissal as the expected discipline is more complex. In particular, when police misconduct includes very serious forms, such as stealing from a crime scene or abusing deadly force, the police officers expected dismissal and, if they perceive that the police administration will administer some intermediate discipline instead, they would not be willing to report. In all other examples of police misconduct in our questionnaire, the expectation of a dismissal compared to any intermediate discipline resulted in police officers' increased willingness to adhere to the code of silence. Police officers viewed dismissal in such cases as an inappropriate discipline and, in turn, decided that they should not report a fellow police officer for an act or omission that might result in dismissal. Indeed, in many of these cases, including those tied to organizational deviance and interpersonal deviance, dismissal is an unlikely outcome for a first-time rule-violator. A lesson for police administrators is that they should weigh very careful which violations of official rules should be career-ending. "Getting it right" and communicating so to the police officers should help them curtail the code of silence.

Our results demonstrate that the severity of the expected discipline matters, but it is not the only consideration that matters; its perceived fairness does too. When the expected discipline is perceived as too harsh, police officers might be more willing to adhere to the code of silence. Our findings show substantial evidence of the theoretical model of simple justice at work, fitting well with the results of extant research (e.g., Datzer et al., 2019; Kutnjak Ivković & Klockars, 1998; Kutnjak Ivković et al., 2016; Kutnjak Ivković & Shelley, 2007, 2010). The first question for police administrators to answer is whether police officers are accurately predicting the discipline that their police agency would mete out. In case they are, then the discussion should be focused on why they perceive such discipline as too harsh. Police administrators may discover that the conditions have changed since the official rules were established and that the less harsh discipline could fulfill the disciplinary goals. Alternatively, the police officers should be taught why such misconduct should be disciplined with the discipline they perceived originally as too harsh.

We have also explored how respondents' evaluations of expected discipline as too lenient are linked with their willingness to stick to the code of silence. Prior research has mostly indicated that there is no strong relationship between assessments of discipline as too lenient and the respondents' willingness to report misconduct (e.g., Datzer et al., 2019; Kutnjak Ivković & Klockars, 1998; Kutnjak Ivković et al., 2016; Kutnjak Ivković & Sauerman, 2013; Kutnjak Ivković & Shelley, 2005, 2007, 2010). In about one-half of the scenarios we also found that the data fit the model of discipline indifference, but in the rest of the scenarios in our full models, we found that, compared to the respondents who evaluated discipline as fair, the respondents who evaluated discipline as too lenient were less likely to say that they would stick to the code of silence. The officers in this subgroup advocated for more severe discipline than they expected their agency to mete out and were also more likely to say that they would report. Assuming that their answers were not a consequence of their self-serving bias, future research could explore their views in more detail.

We also expanded the results to look at the effects of organizational justice on the decision to adhere to the code of silence. There is a consistent relationship between organizational justice and workplace deviance (Colquitt et al., 2005), and failing to report the misconduct of others—especially in policing—is a form of misconduct. Thus, we would have expected to see a consistent negative relationship between organizational justice and adherence to the code of silence. However, the effect of organizational justice on the respondents' decision whether to report misconduct could be best described as inconsistent across models. Even in the more parsimonious models presented in Chap. 4, we only saw a significant negative effect in 3 of the 12 scenarios and a positive effect in 2 of the 12 scenarios, while in the majority of them—8 out of 12 scenarios—there was no relationship between organizational justice and the expressed willingness to adhere to the code of silence. After including all of the additional variables in this chapter, significant negative effects of organizational justice were present in six scenarios, significant positive effects in four, and there were none in the remaining two. For all of the corruption scenarios, the effect of organizational justice on adherence to the code of silence is negative, but varied between the other scenarios. While organizational justice increases adherence to the code of silence in certain scenarios, this should not be construed to mean that police executives do not need to enhance organizational justice in their organizations. Again, enhancing organizational justice may be a proverbial mixed bag, but the deleterious effects of enhancing organizational justice may be outweighed by the positive effects. Further research is needed to unpack the potentially complicated relationship of organizational justice which has been suggested by other scholars in this area (Nagin & Telep, 2017).

The conflicting results here suggest that the true effect of organizational justice may be more complicated than prior research leads on. These differences could be a result of the fact that we use organizational justice to predict adherence to the code of silence (i.e., failing to do something), whereas most prior research has looked at decisions to affirmatively engage in misconduct (see generally Culquitt et al., 2005). This subtle difference may be important and may not be as contrary to prior research as it initially seems. Recently, the importance of strengthening perceptions of organizational justice in police agencies has become increasingly ubiquitous because of the positive effects that come from this elevated sense of organizational justice (Wolfe & Lawson, 2020). An agency could still see the benefits of organizational justice in the behavior of officers consistent with prior research, but that organizational justice may inconsistently influence officers' willingness to report the misconduct of others. In essence, the bolstered organizational justice may change how officers behave, but does not necessarily overcome fundamental elements of the police culture (i.e., adherence to the code of silence). Additional research is needed in this area to determine the veracity of this conjecture.

Finally, we turn to the effects of self-legitimacy. There is a growing body of literature which suggests that self-legitimacy can positively affect the attitudes and behaviors of police officers (Concepcion, 2021). Our work tried to extend the study of self-legitimacy into the study of police integrity, specifically the code of silence. The results here suggest that self-legitimacy yields an inconsistent effect across scenarios—regardless of whether it is only included in the model with other police integrity variables (i.e., Chap. 5) or along with the inclusion of additional relevant factors (i.e., this chapter). At first blush, the results from the full models presented in this chapter suggest that self-legitimacy may not be a desirable trait to instill in police officers, at least if the goal is to maximize willingness to report the misconduct of others. After all, in 7 of the 12 scenarios self-legitimacy significantly increased adherence to the code of silence, while exerting a significant negative effect in four of the scenarios.

Self-legitimacy increased adherence to the code of silence in the corruption scenarios, but exerted differential effects across other types of scenarios. The results for the excessive force scenarios are particularly diverse; self-legitimacy increases adherence to the code of silence in the scenario depicting verbal abuse of a citizen, yet it decreases the adherence to the code in the scenario depicting a failure to report a beating. These results are both supportive and contrary to prior research which consistently found that officers' self-legitimacy is associated with lower willingness to use force and a greater desire to build positive partnerships with the community (Bradford & Quinton, 2014). However, these differences may not be inconsistent with prior research. Self-legitimacy talks about the confidence that officers have in the authority vested in them, which is created in dialogue with multiple constituencies (Nix & Wolfe, 2017). This may mean that—all else being equal—self-legitimacy could be the highest in those officers who have internalized the police subculture the strongest. For instance, self-legitimacy may exert a positive effect in the case of the verbal abuse of the motorist, because in this scenario the motorist's actions could make him/her an "asshole" that needs to be treated differently (Van Maanen, 1978). Thus, the response from the officer depicted could be consistent with the expectations of an officer with self-legitimacy, whereas the actions of the officer who fails to report the beating of a suspect may be seen as something the officer with self-legitimacy would not do. The same potential explanation can be used to justify the inconsistent effects seen across other scenarios, apart from the corruption scenarios. Clearly, additional work on self-legitimacy is needed to address these issues and to determine whether the effects of self-legitimacy are generalizable from agency to agency, given the differences in organizational culture and climate.

The goal of our book has been to study factors that could be related to the police officers' code of silence that exists in every police agency and to provide evidence-based suggestions for police administrators regarding different ways to curtail the code of silence. Our results vividly demonstrate that what police agency does or does not do—from the establishment of the official rules and their enforcement to the way supervisors treat their subordinates—directly affects police officers' willingness to remain a part of the code of silence. Although the traditional police integrity factors, such as the evaluations of misconduct seriousness, severity of expected discipline, and the peers' willingness to report misconduct, perform critical roles in shaping the code of silence, our results demonstrate that the expansion of the traditional approach through the organizational justice elements, discipline fairness, and self-legitimacy provide further valuable information about what makes police officers decide to protect misconduct in silence.

References

Adams, J. S. (1963). Toward an understanding of inequity. *Journal of Abnormal and Social Psychology, 67*, 422–436.
Adams, J. S. (1965). Inequity in social exchange. *Advances in Experimental Social Psychology, 2*, 267–299.

References

Akers, R. L., & Sellers, C. S. (2013). *Criminological theories: Introduction, evaluation, and application.* Oxford University Press.

Angrist, J. D., & Pischke, J. S. (2008). *Mostly harmless econometrics: An Empiricist's companion.* Princeton University Press.

Aronfreed, J. (1965). *Punishment learning and internalization: Some parameters of reinforcement and cognition.* Paper presented at the biennial meeting of the Society for Research in Child Development, Minneapolis.

Arvey, R. D., & Ivancevich, J. M. (1980). Punishment in organizations: A review, propositions, and research suggestions. *The Academy of Management Review, 5,* 123–132.

Barker, R. (2001). *Legitimating identities: The self-presentations of rulers and subjects.* Cambridge University Press.

Bittner, E. (1970). *The functions of the police in modern society: A review of background factors, current practices, and possible role models.* Chevy Chase: National Institute of Mental Health, Center for Studies of Crime and Delinquency.

Bottoms, E. A., & Tankebe, J. (2012). Beyond procedural justice: A dialogic approach to legitimacy in criminal justice. *Journal of Criminal Law and Criminology, 102,* 119–170.

Bradford, B., & Quinton, P. (2014). Self-legitimacy, police culture and support for democratic policing in an English constabulary. *British Journal of Criminology, 54,* 1023–1046.

Cheloukhine, S., Kutnjak Ivković, S., Haq, Q., & Haberfeld, M. R. (2015). Police integrity in Russia. In S. Kutnjak Ivković & M. Haberfeld (Eds.), *Police integrity across the world.* Springer.

Cohen-Charash, Y., & Spector, P. E. (2001). The role of justice in organisations: A meta-analysis. *Organisational Behaviour & Human Decision Processes, 86,* 278–321.

Colquitt, J. A., Greenberg, J., & Zapata-Phelan, C. P. (2005). What is organizational justice? A historical overview. In J. Greenberg & J. A. Colquitt (Eds.), *Handbook of organizational justice.* Lawrence Erlbaum Associates.

Concepcion, S. (2021). *A review of self-legitimacy in policing* (Thesis). Retrieved 26 August 2021, from https://dspace.wlu.edu/handle/11021/35403

Datzer, D., Kutnjak Ivković, S., Mujanović, E., & Morgan, S. (2019). A complex relation between the code of silence and education. In S. Kutnjak Ivković & M. Haberfeld (Eds.), *Exploring police integrity: Novel approaches to police integrity theory and methodology.* Springer.

Deutsch, M. (1975). Equity, equality, and need: What determines which value will be used as the basis of distributive justice? *Journal of Social Issues, 31,* 137–149.

Deutsch, M. (1985). *Distributive justice.* Yale University Press.

Feeley, M. M. (1978). Pleading guilty in lower courts. *Law & Society Review, 13,* 461–466.

Festinger, L. (1954). A theory of social comparison processes. *Human Relations, 7,* 117–140.

Fridell, L. A., Maskály, J., & Donner, C. M. (2021). The relationship between organizational justice and police officer attitudes toward misconduct. *Policing and Society.* https://doi.org/10.1080/10439463.2020.1834558

Gary, A. L. (1971). Industrial absenteeism: An evaluation of three methods of treatment. *The Personnel Journal, 50,* 352–353.

Gau, J. M., & Paoline, E. A. (2020). Police officers' self-assessed legitimacy: A theoretical extension and empirical test. *Justice Quarterly, 38,* 276–300.

Greenberg, J. (1987). A taxonomy of organizational justice theories. *Academy of Management Review, 12,* 9–22.

Greenberg, J. (2009). Promote procedural and interactional justice to enhance individual and organizational outcomes. In E. A. Locke (Ed.), *Handbook of principles of organizational behavior: Indispensable knowledge for evidence-based management* (2nd ed., pp. 255–271). Wiley.

Haberfeld, M. R. (2004). The heritage of police misconduct: The case of the polish police. In C. B. Klockars, S. Kutnjak Ivković, & M. R. Haberfeld (Eds.), *The contours of police integrity* (pp. 95–210). Sage Publications.

Hickman, M. J., Piquero, A. R., Powell, Z. A., & Greene, J. (2016). Expanding the measurement of police integrity. *Policing: An International Journal of Police Strategies & Management, 39*(2), 246–267.

Khechumyan, A., & Kutnjak Ivković, S. (2015). Police integrity in Armenia. In S. Kutnjak Ivković & M. Haberfeld (Eds.), *Police integrity across the world*. Springer.

Klockars, C. B., Kutnjak Ivković, S., & Haberfeld, M. R. (Eds.). (2004). *The contours of police integrity*. Sage.

Klockars, C. B., Kutnjak Ivković, S., & Haberfeld, M. R. (2006). *Enhancing police integrity*. Springer.

Klockars, C. B., Kutnjak Ivković, S., Harver, W. E., and M. R. Haberfeld (1997). The measurement of police integrity. Final Report Submitted to the U.S. Department of Justice, Office of Justice Programs, National Institute of Justice.

Klockars, C. B., Kutnjak Ivković, S., Harver, W. E., & Haberfeld, M. R. (2000). *The measurement of police integrity. Research in brief. U.S. Department of Justice, Office of Justice Programs, National Institute of Justice*. Government Printing Office.

Knapp Commission. (1972). *Report of the commission to investigate allegations of police corruption and the city's anti-corruption procedures*. George Braziller.

Kutnjak Ivković, S. (2015). Studying police integrity. In S. Kutnjak Ivković & M. Haberfeld (Eds.), *Police integrity across the world*. Springer.

Kutnjak Ivković, S., & Haberfeld, M. R. (2015). A comparative perspective on police integrity. In S. Kutnjak Ivković & M. Haberfeld (Eds.), *Police integrity across the world*. Springer.

Kutnjak Ivković, S., & Haberfeld, M. R. (Eds.). (2019). *Exploring police integrity: Novel approaches to police integrity theory and methodology*. Springer.

Kutnjak Ivković, S., Haberfeld, M., & Peacock, R. (2013). Rainless west: The integrity survey's role in agency accountability. *Police Quarterly, 16*(2), 148–176.

Kutnjak Ivković, S., Peacock, R., & Haberfeld, M. (2016). Does discipline fairness matter for the police code of silence? Answers from the U.S. supervisors and line officers. *Policing: An International Journal of Police Strategies and Management, 39*(2), 354–369.

Kutnjak Ivković, S., Haberfeld, M., & Peacock, R. (2018). Decoding the code of silence. *Criminal Justice Policy Review, 29*(2), 172–189.

Kutnjak Ivković, S., Haberfeld, M., & Peacock, R. (2019). Overlapping shades of blue: Exploring police officer, supervisor, and administrator cultures of police integrity. In S. Kutnjak Ivković & M. Haberfeld (Eds.), *Exploring police integrity*. Springer.

Kutnjak Ivković, S., & Khechumyan, A. (2013). The state of police integrity in Armenia: Findings from the police integrity survey. *Policing: An International Journal of Police Strategies and Management, 36*(1), 70–90. https://doi.org/10.1108/13639511311302489

Kutnjak Ivković, S., & Klockars, C. B. (1998). The code of silence and the Croatian police. In M. Pagon (Ed.), *Policing in central and Eastern Europe: Organizational, managerial, and human resource aspects* (pp. 329–347). College of Police and Security Studies.

Kutnjak Ivković, S., & Sauerman, A. (2013). Curtailing the code of silence among the south African police. *Policing: An International Journal of Police Strategies and Management, 36*(1), 175–198.

Kutnjak Ivković, S., & Shelley, T. O. (2005). The Bosnian police and police integrity: A continuing story. *European Journal of Criminology, 2*(4), 428–454.

Kutnjak Ivković, S., & Shelley, T. O. (2007). Police integrity and the Czech police officers. *International Journal of Comparative and Applied Criminal Justice, 31*(1), 21–49.

Kutnjak Ivković, S., & Shelley, T. O. (2010). The code of silence and disciplinary fairness: A comparison of Czech police supervisor and line officer views. *Policing: An International Journal of Police Strategies and Management, 33*(3), 548–574.

Lerner, M. J. (1977). The justice motive: Some hypotheses as to its origins and forms. *Journal of Personality, 45*, 1–52.

Lim, H., & Sloan, J. J. (2016). Police officer integrity: A partial replication and extension. *Policing: An International Journal of Police Strategies & Management, 39*(2), 284–301.

References

Lobnikar, B., & Meško, G. (2015). Police integrity in Slovenia. In S. Kutnjak Ivković & M. Haberfeld (Eds.), *Police integrity across the world*. Springer.

Long, M., Cross, J. E., Shelley, T. O., & Kutnjak Ivković, S. (2013). The normative order of reporting police misconduct: Examining the roles of offense seriousness, legitimacy, and fairness. *Social Psychology Quarterly, 76*(3), 242–267.

Meško, G., Hacin, R., & Tankebe, J. (2017). Self-legitimacy, organisational commitment and commitment to fair treatment of prisoners: An empirical study of prison officers in Slovenia. *European Journal of Crime, Criminal Law, and Criminal Justice, 25*, 11–30.

Mollen Commission. (1994). *[Mollen Commission] New York City Commission to investigate allegations of Police corruption and the anti-corruption procedures of the Police Department (1994)*. Commission Report. New York: Author.

Moreto, W. D., Gau, J. M., Singh, R., Belecky, M., McVey, D., Avino, F. S., & Ononino, A. B. (2021). *Self-legitimacy among rangers in Africa, Asia, and Latin America: An empirical assessment*. Biological Conservation.

Nagin, D. S., & Telep, C. W. (2017). Procedural justice and legal compliance. *Annual Review of Law and Social Science, 13*, 5–28.

Nix, J., & Wolfe, S. E. (2017). The impact of negative publicity on police self-legitimacy. *Justice Quarterly, 34*, 84–108.

Pagon, M., & Lobnikar, B. (2000). Comparing supervisor and line officer opinions about the code of silence: The case of Slovenia. In M. Pagon (Ed.), *Policing in central and Eastern Europe: Ethics, integrity, and human rights* (pp. 197–209). Ljubljana.

Parke, R. D. (1972). Some effects of punishment on children's behavior. In W. W. Hartup (Ed.), *The young child: Reviews of research*. National Association for the Education of Children.

Peacock, R., Prpić, M., Kutnjak Ivković, S., Cajner Mraović, I., & Božović, V. (2020). Shades of blue: Exploring the code of silence in Croatia and Serbia. *International Journal of Comparative and Applied Criminal Justice*. Online first. https://doi.org/10.1080/01924036.2020.1824872

Porter, L. E., & Prenzler, T. (2016). The code of silence and ethical perceptions: Exploring police officer unwillingness to report misconduct. *Policing: An International Journal of Police Strategies & Management, 39*(2), 370–386.

Rosen, B., & Jardee, T. H. (1974). Factors influencing disciplinary judgements. *Journal of Applied Psychology, 59*, 327–331.

Tankebe, J. (2010). Public confidence in the police: Testing the effects of public experiences of police corruption in Ghana. *British Journal of Criminology, 50*, 296–319.

Tankebe, J. (2014). 'The making of democracy's champions': Understanding police support for democracy in Ghana. *Criminology and Criminal Justice, 14*, 25–43.

Tankebe, J., & Meško, G. (2015). Police self-legitimacy, use of force, and pro-organizational behavior in Slovenia. In G. Meško & J. Tankebe (Eds.), *Trust and legitimacy in criminal justice* (pp. 261–270). Springer.

Vallmüür, B. (2015). Police integrity in Estonia. In S. Kutnjak Ivković & M. Haberfeld (Eds.), *Police integrity across the world*. Springer.

Van Droogenbroeck, F., Spruyt, B., Kutnjak Ivković, S., & Haberfeld, M. R. (2019). The effects of ethics training on police integrity. In S. Kutnjak Ivković & M. Haberfeld (Eds.), *Exploring police integrity: Novel approaches to police integrity theory and methodology*. Springer.

Van Maanen, J. (1978). The asshole. In P. K. Manning & J. Van Maanen (Eds.), *Policing: A view from the street* (pp. 221–238). Goodyear Publishing.

Walster, E., & Walster, G. W. (1975). Equity and social justice. *Journal of Social Issues, 31*, 21–44.

Weinstein, L. (1969). Decreased sensitivity to punishment. *Psychonomic Science, 14*, 264–265.

Weisburd, D. (2010). Justifying the use of non-experimental methods and disqualifying the use of randomized controlled trials: Challenging folklore in evaluation research in crime and justice. *Journal of Experimental Criminology, 6*(2), 209–227.

Weisburd, D., Cave, B., & Piquero, A. R. (2016). How do criminologists interpret statistical explanation of crime? A review of quantitative modeling in published studies. In A. R. Piquero (Ed.), *Handbook of criminological theory*. Wiley.

Westmarland, L. (2006). Police ethics and integrity: Breaking the blue code of silence. *Policing and Society, 15*(2), 145–165.

Westley, W. (1970). *Violence and the police: A sociological study of law, custom, and morality.* MIT Press.

Wolfe, S., & Lawson, S. (2020). The organizational justice effect among criminal justice employees: A meta-analysis. *Criminology, 58*(4), 619–644.

Wu, G., & Makin, D. (2019). The quagmire that is an unwillingness to report: Situating the code of silence within the Chinese police context. *Criminal Justice and Behavior, 46*, 608–627.

Open Access This chapter is licensed under the terms of the Creative Commons Attribution 4.0 International License (http://creativecommons.org/licenses/by/4.0/), which permits use, sharing, adaptation, distribution and reproduction in any medium or format, as long as you give appropriate credit to the original author(s) and the source, provide a link to the Creative Commons license and indicate if changes were made.

The images or other third party material in this chapter are included in the chapter's Creative Commons license, unless indicated otherwise in a credit line to the material. If material is not included in the chapter's Creative Commons license and your intended use is not permitted by statutory regulation or exceeds the permitted use, you will need to obtain permission directly from the copyright holder.

Index

A
Abolish the police, 2
Audience legitimacy, 78
    See also Legitimacy

B
Blue curtain, *see* Code of silence
Blue wall of silence, *see* Code of silence

C
Christopher Commission, 1–5
Code of silence, 4, 18
    contours, 26
    control mechanisms, 21
    definition, 4–5
    empirical studies, 19
    excessive force, 7, 8, 29, 50–51, 68, 88, 107
    interpersonal deviance, 30
    measurement, 7, 27–30, 48–52, 62–64, 83–85
    misconduct seriousness, 20, 23
    organizational deviance, 29
    police corruption, 26, 27
    police integrity, 11
    theory of police integrity, 5, 7, 28
    violation of official rules, 27, 30
Compliance, *see* Rule compliance
Consent decree, 2
    See also Pattern and practice lawsuits
Control mechanisms
    code of silence, 6, 9, 21, 81, 82
    discipline, 6, 9, 21, 81
    official rules, 6, 9, 21, 81
    rule violations, 6, 111
Curran Committee, 2

D
Defund the police, 2
Discipline
    appropriate, 9, 21, 23, 40, 43, 103, 111
    and code of silence, 37–53
    and disciplinary fairness, 37–53
    dismissal, 24, 28, 30, 43, 50, 51, 69, 111
    expected, 18, 21, 23, 24, 30–32, 38–47, 50–52, 62, 63, 83, 84, 95, 103, 111, 112, 114
    fairness, 37–53
    harsh, 44, 48–51, 64, 105, 112
    intermediate, 28–31, 49, 67, 87, 105, 106, 111
    lenient, 44, 46, 48–51
    measurement, 40–41
    and organizational justice, 97–99, 107–108
    rule violations, 111
    and self-legitimacy, 101
    theory of police integrity, 38–41
Disciplinary fairness
    and code of silence, 37–53
    deterrence, 39, 41, 47, 52
    distributive justice, 58, 63, 97–98
    excessive force, 50–51
    harsh discipline, 44, 48–51
    interpersonal deviance, 51, 69, 89, 108
    justice, 97–99
    lenient discipline, 44, 46, 48–51
    measurement, 40, 42–44, 48–52

Disciplinary fairness (*cont.*)
  organizational deviance, 29, 51, 68, 89, 107–108
  organizational justice, 97–99, 107–108
  police corruption, 27–28, 48–50, 66–68, 86–88, 104–105
  police integrity, 38–41
  and self-legitimacy, 101
  theoretical approaches, 39–40, 79
  theory of police integrity, 37–41, 48–52
Discipline fairness, 38, 39, 98
  See also Disciplinary fairness
Distributive justice, 97, 98
  and disciplinary fairness, 37–53
  interactional justice, 63, 99
  measurement, 63, 97, 104
  organizational justice, 58, 63, 67, 97–98
  and police integrity, 38–41
  procedural justice, 58, 63, 99
  and self-legitimacy, 101
  theory of police integrity, 63, 97, 98

E
Education, 10, 21, 22, 24, 25, 44, 64, 104

F
Fitzgerald inquiry, 3, 4

G
Gender, 10, 21, 24, 25, 44, 64, 104

H
Helfand Investigation, 2
High-profile incidents, 2

I
Informational justice
  interactional justice, 63, 99
  organizational justice, 58
  procedural justice, 58
Interactional justice
  and disciplinary fairness, 64
  distributive justice, 63
  measurement, 63
  organizational justice, 63, 99
  and police integrity, 62, 65, 99
  procedural justice, 58, 63, 99
  and self-legitimacy, 99

J
Job performance, 59, 64
Job satisfaction, 57–60

K
Knapp Commission, 2, 109

L
Legitimacy
  audience legitimacy, 77–79, 81
  police-community partnerships, 81
  and police integrity, 85–90
  self-legitimacy, 77–92, 99–101
Length of service, 10, 21, 24, 44, 64, 104
Lexow Committee, 2

M
Mollen Commission, 2–4, 18, 109

O
Official rules
  code of silence, 6, 9, 18, 20–21, 23, 38, 39, 43, 62, 63, 103, 110–112, 114
  discipline, 6, 9, 18, 21, 23, 39, 62, 63, 103, 110–112
  disciplinary fairness, 38, 39, 43–44, 103
  organizational justice, 20, 62, 63, 110, 112
  police integrity, 6, 18, 20, 23, 38, 39, 81, 103, 110
  police misconduct, 6, 18, 20, 24, 38, 110, 111
  violations of rules, 6, 23, 39, 43, 63, 103, 111
  See also Rule compliance
Organizational commitment, 59, 60, 100
Organizational justice, 11, 58, 64, 98
  and code of silence, 58, 61–62, 65, 67
  and discipline fairness, 39, 97–99
  distributive justice, 58, 63, 97, 98, 105
  informational justice, 58
  interpersonal justice, 58, 97
  measurement, 27–30, 48–52, 62–64, 83–85
  procedural justice, 58–61, 63, 99
  and self-legitimacy, 99, 100

P
Pattern and practice lawsuits, 2
Peers, *see* Police officers

Police corruption, 4, 5, 7–9, 11, 12, 18, 19, 22, 26–28, 31, 42, 45, 48, 50, 62, 65–68, 70, 83, 86–88, 102, 104–105
Police culture, 3, 5, 17, 31, 109, 110, 113
  code of silence, 3, 5, 31, 81
  Knapp Commission, 2, 109
  Mollen Commission, 2–4, 18, 109
  norms, 3, 7
  peers, 31, 82, 88, 110
  self-legitimacy, 82, 113, 114
  supervisors, 3, 82
Police integrity
  appropriate discipline, 9, 24–25, 40, 103
  code of silence, 5–7, 17
  definition, 6
  dimensions, 6, 9, 20, 40, 81–82
  discipline fairness, 38–41, 48–52
  expected discipline, 21, 24, 30–32, 41, 43, 47, 50
  excessive force, 5, 7, 8, 18, 22, 23, 29, 49, 50, 68, 85, 87, 88, 107
  interactional deviance, 79, 82
  measurement, 27–30, 48–52, 62–64, 83–85
  misconduct seriousness, 20, 22, 23, 38, 43, 62, 63, 95, 103, 110, 114
  organizational deviance, 8, 18, 19, 22, 26–30, 42, 46, 47, 49, 51, 65–69, 71, 89, 106–108
  and organizational justice, 59–61, 63, 99
  police corruption, 18, 19, 26–28, 45, 48–50, 66–68, 86–88, 104–105
  and self-legitimacy, 85–90, 104–109
  theory of police integrity, 5–7, 9, 17–32
Police integrity approach
  discipline, 38–41, 97–99
  excessive force, 18, 22, 23, 29, 49, 50, 68, 85, 87, 88, 107
  interpersonal deviance, 79, 82
  informational deviance, 58
  measurement, 27–30, 48–52, 62–64, 83–85
  misconduct seriousness, 20, 22, 23, 38, 43, 62, 63, 95, 103, 110
  police corruption, 18, 19, 26–28, 45, 48–50, 66–68, 86–88, 104–105
  theory, 5–7, 9, 17–32
  violation of rules, 20, 23, 43, 63, 103, 111
  See also Theory of police integrity
Police integrity theory, 11, 18, 28, 38, 77, 81–84, 97, 102, 108
  See also Theory of police integrity
Police legitimacy, 77–92
Police misconduct, 1, 2
  excessive force, 18, 22, 23, 29, 49, 50, 68, 85, 87, 88, 107
  interpersonal deviance, 79, 82
  official rules, 6, 20, 23, 39, 43, 103
  organizational deviance, 18, 81
  police corruption, 21–22
  police integrity, 20, 21, 23, 63, 81, 111
Police officers, 9
  code of silence, 4–12, 20–22, 27–29, 38, 39, 58, 61, 68
  organizational deviance, 29–30, 52, 68, 69, 89, 108
  police culture, 91, 110
  self-legitimacy, 80–90
  supervisors, 10, 58–61, 82, 89, 99, 100, 114
Police reform, 2, 3, 18
Police subculture, 5
  See also Police culture
Procedural justice
  discipline fairness, 41, 42, 46, 56
  distributive justice, 58, 63, 97–98
  internal justice, 60
  interactional justice, 63, 99
  organizational justice, 59–61, 63, 99
  and police integrity, 40–42
  and self-legitimacy, 78, 81, 82
Punishment, 98, 99
  See also Discipline

Q

Questionnaire
  appropriate discipline, 9, 21, 23, 43, 103
  expected discipline, 21, 24, 38–47, 52, 62, 112
  measurement, 7, 22, 40, 42, 62, 83, 102
  misconduct seriousness, 20, 23, 38, 62, 63
  police corruption questionnaire, 7, 19, 22
  police integrity questionnaire, 7, 9, 19, 22, 31, 42, 62, 83, 102
  theory of police integrity, 19, 21–25
  violation of rules, 21, 22, 62, 83, 111
  willingness to report, 11, 21, 23, 25, 26, 38–41, 44–48, 58, 63, 68, 82–85

R

Rank, 3, 5, 24–26, 29, 43
Recruitment and selection, 60
Reimagine the police, 2
Rule compliance
  code of silence, 59, 60
  discipline, 59
  distributive justice, 63
  organizational justice, 59

Rule compliance (*cont.*)
  peers, 82
  procedural justice, 59
  supervisors, 59–61

S
Seabury Report, 2
Scenarios
  excessive force, 7, 8, 19, 22, 23, 29, 31, 42, 45, 49, 50, 65, 68, 71, 83, 88, 89, 102, 104, 107, 113
  interpersonal deviance, 7, 8, 11, 19, 22, 27, 30, 42, 45, 47, 51, 52, 62, 65, 68, 70, 71, 83, 85, 89, 108
  organizational deviance, 7, 8, 11, 12, 17–19, 22, 27–31, 46, 51, 68, 71, 83, 89, 102, 107
  police corruption, 7, 8, 11, 19, 22, 27, 31, 42, 45, 48, 50, 62, 70, 83, 86, 104
  police integrity, 9, 19, 48, 50, 51, 62, 88
  questionnaire, 7, 9, 19, 22, 24, 25, 31, 40, 42, 62, 63, 83, 84, 102, 111
  theory of police integrity, 9, 20–31
Self-legitimacy, 77, 78, 99
  and code of silence, 77–92
  definition of, 78–79, 101
  excessive force, 83, 85, 87–90
  interpersonal deviance, 83, 85–90
  measurement, 84
  organizational deviance, 83, 85–87, 89
  police attitudes and behavior, 80
  police corruptionm, 83
  and police integrity, 85–90
  and police integrity theory, 82
  theoretical approaches, 79
Subculture, *see* Police culture

Supervisors, 3, 10, 25–29, 48, 59–61, 64–68, 82, 86–90, 99, 100
Survey, *see* Questionnaire

T
Theory of police integrity, 5, 7
  code of silence, 41, 61, 81–82
  and disciplinary fairness, 97–99, 101
  excessive force, 18, 22, 23, 29, 49, 50, 68, 85, 87, 88, 107
  interpersonal deviance, 42, 45, 47, 51, 52, 62, 65, 68, 70, 71, 83, 85, 89, 108
  measurement, 22, 27
  misconduct seriousness, 20, 22, 23, 38, 43, 62, 63, 95, 103, 110
  organizational deviance, 18, 19, 22, 26–30, 42, 46, 47, 49, 51, 65–69, 71, 89, 106–108
  and organizational justice, 96–110
  police integrity questionnaire, 7, 9, 19, 22, 31, 42, 62, 83, 102
  police corruption, 18, 19, 26–28, 45, 48–50, 66–68, 86–88, 104–105
  police corruption questionnaire, 7, 19, 22
  and self-legitimacy, 104–109
  violation of rules, 20, 23, 43, 63, 103, 111

V
Vignettes, *see* Scenarios, questionnaire

W
Wood Royal Commission, 4
Work attitudes, 59

The manufacturer's authorised representative in the EU is Springer Nature Customer Service Centre GmbH, Europaplatz 3, 69115 Heidelberg, Germany. If you have any concerns regarding our products, please contact ProductSafety@springernature.com

Printed and bound by CPI Group (UK) Ltd, Croydon, CR0 4YY

25/03/2026

02078233-0001